MICHAEL JORDAN

MICHAEL JORDAN

Chip Lovitt

SCHOLASTIC INC.
New York   Toronto   London   Auckland   Sydney
Mexico City   New Delhi   Hong Kong

Photo credits

Acknowledgments

The author wishes to thank the following people for their cooperation and assistance: David Bridgers, Buzz Peterson, Kenneth McLaurin, Janice Hardy, Bety Greer, Liam O'Mahony, the Chicago Bulls Media Services Department, and Michael Jordan who took the time out from his busy 1991-1992 basketball season to graciously and enthusiastically answer my questions.

For my favorite basketball
player, Keith Lovitt

Contents

MICHAEL JORDAN

Introduction

It will always be remembered as one of the great introductions in sports. The pregame warm-ups and shoot-arounds are done. The court has been cleared. Suddenly, the lights in Chicago's United Center go off. The arena is dark. A sellout crowd of more than 23,000 erupts in an ear-splitting chorus of whistles, screams, and shouts. As the sound system pours out a pulsing rock beat, bright lights swirl around the arena, cutting through the darkness. A huge, angry-looking red bull's face lights up the scoreboard and blinks down at the cheering crowd.

"And now," the announcer says, "the starting lineup for your World Champion Chicago Bulls." The noise level rises higher as the first four starters are introduced. Then the cheers grow deafening as the last starter trots onto the court. "At guard, six-foot-six," the announcer calls out, "out of North Carolina . . ." The player's name is drowned out in the din, but no one in the arena —

and no sports fan in the world — needs an introduction to number 23. He is Michael Jordan, the perennial scoring champ of the National Basketball Association and, to many, the best ever to play the game of basketball.

The Bull's pregame ceremony — at noisy old Chicago Stadium, the site of some of Michael's greatest games, or at the United Center — never fails to whip the hometown crowd into a frenzy. It is spectacular, but the real excitement begins when Michael Jordan gets the ball. That's when fans are treated to a dazzling display of dunks, drives, and thrilling three-point shots. And often, by the time the game has ended, there are thousands of fans who would swear they'd seen a man fly.

To Michael Jordan, every game is a challenge, and since boyhood, Mike has liked nothing more than a challenge. Whether he was trying to dunk in his backyard, struggling to make a high school team as a teenager, or trying to win the biggest prize in pro basketball, "Air" Jordan has always risen to the occasion.

Whenever they look up, fans at the United Center get a reminder of how high Michael has taken the Bulls and the game of basketball. Hanging high from the rafters at the United Center are the banners that mark the Bulls' five NBA championships. Nearby are other banners honoring the numbers of the Bulls' all-time best players. And there's already a space reserved for number 23, to commemorate the career of the greatest of them all, Michael Jordan.

Michael Jordan's story is a great one. It is the story of a boy who dreamed of becoming a champion and made the dream come true with years of practice, dedication, and determination — plus a style all his own. There has never been an athlete quite like Michael Jordan and there may never be again.

1
A Lucky Star

Throughout his incredible career, Michael Jordan often said he considered himself lucky. When the Chicago Bulls' superstar talked about being lucky, he wasn't referring to basketball. Hard work, practice, and talent are more responsible for his success in sports than luck. When the Chicago Bulls' superstar guard talked about his good luck, he meant his family and the life they inspired him to lead.

"I learned the value of hard work and persistence from my family," Michael Jordan says. "I was lucky to have parents who care. They gave me guidance and taught me to work hard. I've learned my lessons.

"My family has been my inspiration to succeed," Michael adds. "They were always pushing me and fighting me and helping me become the man I am today."

Michael's mother and father, Deloris and James Jordan, grew up in Rocky Creek and Wallace, two small towns in North Carolina. Appropriately enough, they met at a high school basketball game. James proposed to Deloris in the spring of 1957, and they were married that fall. By the end of 1962, the Jordans had three children, Ronald James, Deloris,and Larry.

James and Deloris were the children of sharecroppers and no strangers to hard work. James was driving a tractor by age 10 and had spent many hours in the fields planting crops and harvesting tobacco leaves in the hot southern sun. Later, James worked for General Electric, first as a forklift operator, then as a mechanic, dispatcher, and eventually equipment supervisor. As a mechanic, James needed to learn something about hydraulics so he could repair automatic transmissions in the trucks he worked on. So he decided to take some night classes in hydraulics in New York City.

"In my family, we try to make things happen, rather than waiting for them to happen. We believe the surest way is to work toward making it happen," James says.

The family drove north and found an apartment in Brooklyn. Deloris was pregnant at the time. She, along with the rest of the Jordans, was eager to return to North Carolina once James's classes were finished and the new baby arrived.

Michael Jeffrey Jordan was born on February 17, 1963, in a Brooklyn hospital. The Jordans took Michael home after three days and when James completed his courses, the family returned to Wallace.

Both parents remember Michael as a happy baby.

6

"Michael was such a jolly baby," Deloris recalled. "He never cried. Just feed him, give him something to play with, and he'd be fine."

"He was a real happy-go-lucky type," James added.

Michael was also a curious and inquisitive child. "Michael was always testing us," James Jordan explained. "If we told him the stove was hot, don't touch, he'd touch it. If there was a wet paint sign, he'd touch the paint to see if it was wet. If there was something to be tried, he was the one to try it."

Occasionally that almost had disastrous results. When he was two, Michael wandered out into the yard to watch his father work on the family car. James had strung together several extension cords from the house. When James wasn't looking, Michael began playing with the wires. Before James could do anything, Michael got a terrible electric shock and was thrown three feet backward.

When Michael was five, he had another accident that could have ended his basketball career before it had even begun. Michael had been told over and over that he was too young to play with his father's ax. Still, he picked it up when no one was looking and began chopping a piece of wood.

"I didn't have any shoes on. Being from the country, you don't always wear shoes," Michael said. "So I'm chopping little bits and pieces of wood and I accidentally missed the wood and caught half my big toe. I'm yelling and screaming. I'm five years old and I don't know what to do. I

7

ran into the house and my parents drove me to a doctor."

Michael's toe healed completely, but James never forgot the incident. "Every time I fall in a game now," Michael joked, "my father says, 'You shouldn't have played with that ax.' "

When Michael was seven, his parents moved to Wilmington, North Carolina, a sleepy port city located near the Atlantic coast. Wilmington, with a population of about 40,000, had a small-town feel, and James and Deloris thought it would be an ideal place to bring up their children. With the birth of Michael's sister Roslyn in 1964, there were now five Jordan children. James and Deloris bought 12 acres of land on Gordon Street in a quiet middle-class neighborhood dotted with new homes. There was plenty of room for the kids to play and the large Carolina pines that ringed the property would provide shade from the hot sun.

James built the house himself. It was a neat two-story house with a brick exterior and tan clapboard siding. There was a two-car garage and a screened-in porch where the family could sit and enjoy the warm summer breezes that blew in off the ocean and the coastal waterways nearby.

Deloris eventually went to work at the United Carolina Bank, and she worked hard to advance her career. She began as a teller at a drive-in window, was promoted to head teller, then named head of customer service.

In the Jordans' neighborhood, black and white families lived together, side by side. The next-door neighbors, Ann and Mathis Teacher, were white and the two families often helped each other out with baby-sitting and other tasks. Even though Michael had been born in the midst of the civil rights era, the schools the Jordan kids attended had integrated largely without incident. James and Deloris taught their children early on that all people deserved dignity and respect.

Despite being a bit shy, Michael made friends easily. He was closest to his brother Larry and their one-year age difference made them natural playmates. Michael also made friends with the kids in the neighborhood. One of his best friends was David Bridgers, a white boy who met Michael when the two boys played Little League baseball together.

Baseball, not basketball, was Michael's first love. Michael was average height for his age and he found that baseball suited his skills better than basketball, which was Larry's game.

"I met Michael playing baseball," David recalls. "He was a good pitcher. I remember getting up against him the first time. He had a good curve ball and everybody knew it. It broke at you and then broke in over the plate, and I just ran. He struck me out many a time before I finally got hold of one of his pitches. He was good, no doubt about it."

Michael threw two no-hitters in Little League. He was also a good outfielder and hitter. His team represented North Carolina in the regional play-offs of the Little League World Series.

His teammates were not only impressed with Michael's curve ball, but also his confidence.

"When we were in the Little League World Series, this guy said that if any of us hit a home run, he'd take them out for a steak dinner," David says. "Mike stood up in front of all of us and told the guy 'You might as well get one ready.' And I'll be doggoned — Mike hit it out of the park."

The team lost the game to the Texas team 4–3. In the next game, Michael threw a two-hitter, but his team failed to score a run and the team lost 1–0.

Michael graduated to Babe Ruth League baseball and he impressed his coaches with his energy and speed on the basepaths. "Our Babe Ruth League coach called Mike 'Rabbit' because he was always bouncing around and liked to run," David says.

Those were special times for Michael.

"My favorite childhood memory, my greatest achievement," Michael has said, "was when I got the Most Valuable Player award when my Babe Ruth League team won the state championship. That was the first thing I accomplished in my life and you always remember the first. I batted something like .500, hit five home runs in seven games, and pitched a one-hitter to get us to the championship game."

According to David Bridgers, many of the traits that have marked Michael Jordan's adult life were evident as a young boy.

"What I liked most about Mike," he explains, "was his competitiveness. He never went into a game with a halfhearted attitude. If he was going to play, he was going to give it all or he wouldn't play. He loved a challenge, too. We'd go out on hot summer days and play ball all day. We'd take on any team who wanted to play us. Michael could stand up to it. He had tremendous confidence."

According to David, Michael's desire to win was as strong then as it is now. "There's one thing I could say about Mike and I still can say it today. Mike feels that when it's time to go out and win a game, he wants to be the one to do it and make it happen. He thinks he can pull you out of any situation and turn things around at any given time. He had that confidence then and still has it now," David says.

"He was a good-hearted fellow, too. He had a good sense of humor and he'd always laugh and joke around. That's why we hit it off so well."

When they weren't on the baseball field, Michael and David rode their bikes all over town. "We'd ride bikes to practice. When the weekend would come, we'd get on our bikes and ride anywhere and everywhere. We'd ride downtown or we'd ride out by the airport."

Sometimes as a special treat, James Jordan would take Michael, Larry, and David to NASCAR auto races. The boys loved to watch drivers like Richard Petty race the souped-up cars around the track, their wheels squealing and smoking.

David's home life wasn't always happy and he spent many an hour at the Jordan house. "It was a fun place to be," David remembers. "My mother and father split up and going over there and being with them was just like family. His mom and dad were very laid back, but all the Jordans were real

11

individuals and bighearted people. Mike's daddy always said you had to treat others the way you want to be treated. They treated me just like a member of the family."

The Jordans taught their children to be color-blind when it came to race. David recalls, "His mother and father told us many a time that it's not what you see on the outside. It's what's on the inside that counts. It can be white, blue, green, or brown. As long as you have a big heart, you don't see color."

Michael's parents always tried to teach their children positive values. "He had a good home-raising," David remembers. "Mike always knew what to do and what not to do. He always knew right from wrong. They raised me right up among the rest of them and never said word one. But you always knew right from wrong. You could go out and your mother would say 'Have a good time, but don't get in any trouble.' You would have a good time with Mike, but you weren't going to get into any trouble with him."

Michael and David have maintained their friendship to this day. Many of the other friends he would make in his youth would remain close to him even at the height of his pro career. Michael, who often described himself as "a country boy from Carolina" never forgot his roots and never forgot his friends either. Loyalty was something Michael learned to value in his youth and he would carry that trait all the way into his adult life.

2
Battles in the Backyard

Picture this court. By pro basketball standards, it isn't much to look at. Although full-size, the playing surface is grass and hard-packed dirt, not cement or asphalt. The backboards are made from plywood and the rims droop slightly from the impact of countless schoolboy slam dunks. The nets, which once were new and white, now are gray with age and hang torn and shredded.

Despite its appearance, the court was the site of some of Michael Jordan's fiercest games. The court sits in the spacious backyard of the house where Michael grew up. And it was there that Michael learned the basics of the game and where he struggled against his first and toughest opponent, his brother Larry.

James Jordan had played a little basketball in high school, and he passed his love of the game on to his sons. Michael began playing basketball when he was around eight. He and Larry joined a neighborhood league in Wilmington, and the two boys loved the game so much James decided to build them a court of their own.

"At first it was half court," James recalled, "but we kept having more kids over to the house so we made it a full court. Since we had a big backyard, it was easy for me to make them a court."

James Jordan recalled that Michael's basketball talents developed slowly. "His leaping didn't just come. He worked at it. Michael set goals and worked hard to achieve them," James remembers.

Michael may credit his parents with giving him guidance and values, but he says, "I really learned the game of basketball playing against my brother Larry in the backyard."

"Michael first started playing against Larry, who was only five feet seven inches," James explained. "Back then, Larry was a little taller and much stronger than Michael who was still in grade school. Larry would beat Michael mercilessly. As Michael got older, he got bigger — and the games got much closer. That's when the fights started. As long as Larry would beat Michael, everything was okay. Then Michael started beating Larry, and they'd end up rolling on the ground and one of us would have to go out there and break it up. The next day they'd be on the court again, playing like nothing happened."

"It was that big-brother syndrome," David Bridgers adds. "The younger one wants to beat the older one and he's not going to be satisfied until he does. Michael's sport was still baseball at the time, and Larry's was basketball. Larry loved to play and I guess that's where Michael picked up his love of the game. Larry would take Mike out in the back. Larry was small, but had incredible jumping ability. That made up for a lot of height. That's what would get Mike. The games would always be close, and they'd battle back and forth. Larry would come out on top and Mike would just shake his head. He couldn't understand how it was happening. It was a challenge and Mike loved a challenge."

The games with Larry sharpened Michael's skills and, despite his frustration, made him a better player.

"Those backyard games really helped me become the player I am today in a lot of ways," Michael said many years later. "Larry would never give me any slack, never took it easy on me. I learned a lot about being competitive from him."

Michael credits Larry with being a big influence on his style of play. "When you see me play," he said, "you see Larry play."

The backyard court was also the site of Michael's very first dunk.

"I first dunked in my backyard over my brother Larry," Michael recalled. "You have to remember he was a better player when I was growing up, so I was really excited. I still get excited playing Larry. Last time we played, he dunked on me and said, 'Remember who taught you this!' I said to him, 'Remember whose name is on your shoes!' They were Air Jordans," Michael says with a laugh.

Kids from all over the neighborhood would gather at the Jordans' backyard court for impromptu games. Sometimes there would be as many as 20 kids ranging in age from 10 to 18.

"We played neighborhood games for at least two hours every day," Michael said. "On Saturdays we were out there all day. Rainy days? We would still be out there."

Michael particularly enjoyed the challenge of playing against some of his brother's taller friends. It forced him to work even harder. "He couldn't stand to play someone he knew he could beat," David Bridgers notes. "It wasn't a challenge for him. He'd just lose his concentration. But if he were being roughed up or pushed around, especially by bigger boys, he'd really concentrate and play hard.

"He didn't have a very good outside shot then, but you'd still lose when you played him because he wanted the ball so much. Mike would shoot the ball 15 times while you shot 7 or 8 times. He was going to get twice as many shots. That was his ambition. He just wouldn't quit. If he didn't go all out, he wouldn't go out at all."

Michael and Larry were both adventurous kids and sometimes their exploits off the court got them into trouble. When Michael was 12, he and Larry got a little motorbike which they liked to race around the backyard. James had dug a long drainage ditch in the backyard and he told the boys to stay away from it when they rode the bike. One day the boys decided to be daredevils and jump the ditch. They made a homemade ramp and backed up about a hundred feet. The boys raced toward the ramp, picking up speed. The bike flew off the ramp and crashed into the ditch. The boys tumbled off the bike, bruised and bleeding. James sold the motorbike the next day.

While Michael had no hesitation about working hard on his sports skills, he admits, "I was lazy about some things. I never got into mowing the lawn or doing hard jobs."

All the kids in the Jordan family had to do chores, but Michael didn't like physical labor. Sometimes he would purposely mess up his chores, driving his parents crazy. Some of the Jordan kids would work part-time chopping tobacco. Michael hurt his back the first day and never returned.

"Michael is probably the laziest kid I had," James Jordan declared. "He would give every last dime of his allowance to his brothers and sisters and even kids in the neighborhood to do his chores. He was always broke," James said.

"Michael wasn't the easiest child to bring up," Deloris Jordan has said. "We sometimes had to be stern with him."

At D.C. Virgo Junior High, Michael was a popular kid, although some of the older kids teased him about his close-cropped haircut. They nicknamed him "Bald Head" and in lighthearted moments, rubbed their knuckles on his head and gave him noogies. Michael was a guard on the basketball team, a pitcher and an outfielder on the baseball team, and the quarterback of the football team. Baseball, however, was his number-one sport. He was only five feet nine inches, and most of the basketball players were over six feet tall. Michael's parents were both under five feet nine inches, so Michael thought he would be too short to be one of the best players on the team.

Fred Lynch, the basketball coach at the school, was impressed with Michael's dedication. "He was the first to practice and the last to leave. Michael just worked, worked, and worked on his game. He played all the time."

Fred Lynch also noticed Michael's competitive nature. "He hated losing, even then, and that made him work extremely hard when he played any of the sports."

Lynch also noted how supportive Michael's parents were. "They attended all the games and always looked for something positive, whether Michael played well or the team played well."

Michael next attended Laney High School from 1979 to 1981. The school, a low one-story brick building, is nestled in a northern section of Wilmington, North Carolina, on Route 132. The building looks much like any other high school in the country. Walk down a hallway near the gym and you'll come upon a trophy case. In it, mixed in with trophies for football and cheerleading, is a folded up red jersey with the number 23 on it. Below it is a photograph of a smiling, lanky young man in a University of North Carolina basketball uniform, also with the number 23 on it. There's no name on the jersey or the photo, but everyone knows who number 23 is. There is also a plaque.

E.A. Laney H.S.
Division II Champs
1980–81

There, among the dozen names etched into the gold surface, is the name Mike Jordan.

Kenneth McLaurin was the principal of Laney High when Michael attended the school. He first met Michael when Michael was 16. His first impression of Michael was that he was "a typical teenager, even though he was very proficient in sports. He didn't seek any special status or anything else. He was also very playful and had a good sense of humor.

"Michael was not only an excellent basketball player," Kenneth McLaurin notes. "He was a great baseball player, too. We all thought he was a better baseball player than a basketball player. He was also a track star and played junior varsity football."

"In high school I played baseball, football, and track, trying to find the right place for my talents," Michael remembered. "As I grew, I found the best target was the basketball court."

Like many young athletes, Michael hoped to make it as a professional athlete. "I did dream of being in professional sports. I just didn't know whether it would be in baseball or basketball," he says.

One of Michael's biggest heroes when he was in high school was Julius "Dr.J" Erving, the pro basketball player whose fantastic dunks and great moves have made him a sports legend. Erving was

19

one of the first NBA players to utilize his leaping skills to play a high-flying "airborne" game.

"I loved to watch Dr. J," Michael recalls. "He was an inspiration to me, both on and off the court."

Michael joined Laney's jayvee basketball team and played guard. When he got his uniform, Michael chose number 23. His brother Larry, who played on the varsity team, wore number 45. Michael picked 23 as if to say he hoped he would be half as good as his older brother.

Even in those days, Michael would stick out his tongue as he played. He'd picked up the habit from watching his father as a little boy. When James was concentrating on a complicated task like fixing the family car, he'd stick his tongue out. Michael would do the same thing when he was concentrating on his basketball or baseball technique. Soon Michael was doing it all the time.

"I remember my coach telling me I was going to bite my tongue off and find it on the floor. He even tried to get me to wear a mouthpiece when I played. But I just can't do it. I've tried to play with my mouth closed. But if my tongue's not out, I just can't play. I just can't stop it." However, Michael adds, "It's one thing I don't want kids to imitate because it's very dangerous."

Michael made the varsity team as a sophomore, but was cut from the team early in the season. Fred Lynch thought Michael had plenty of potential but would benefit more by playing jayvee ball than by sitting on the varsity bench.

"We thought at the time that it was the best thing for Michael and the basketball program," Fred

Lynch explained. "He was a good ball player, but we didn't think he was good enough yet to really make the contribution we felt we needed."

Michael felt angry and embarrassed that he'd been cut. He returned to the jayvee team where he scored more than 20 points a game. Michael would go to varsity games — as a spectator. Still upset about being cut, he found it hard to root for the team. Years later, Michael admitted that there were times when he wanted Laney's opponents to win. "I guess I wanted them to lose to prove they'd made a mistake by leaving me off the team," he explained.

Late in the season, there was talk that the varsity team would add one more jayvee player to the lineup in case the team made it into the state playoffs. Michael was sure he would be the one. Instead Leroy Smith was called up. The team needed a big man more than it needed another shooting guard, and Smith was six inches taller than Michael. It would not be the last time that Michael's talents were overlooked in favor of a bigger man.

The Laney varsity made it into the playoffs and Michael went with the team — as a substitute manager when the team manager got sick. Michael handed out towels and watched the game from the bench. When the basketball season ended, Michael vowed that he would make the varsity next season no matter how much work it took.

"I made up my mind right then and there that this would never happen again," Michael said. "From that point on, I began working harder than ever on my basketball skills."

Michael shot hoops every opportunity he could. However, when he began cutting classes to work on his game, he was suspended from school. His mother didn't exactly give him the day off, either.

"She parked him outside the teller window and made him study all day," Kenneth McLaurin recalls.

James was tempted to let it go and hope things got better. "But I knew if I didn't do something about it right away, it could only get worse," he states. "I asked Michael what his goal was and he said college. I told him there was no way he was going. He couldn't keep cutting classes and have any hope of going to college. It wasn't going to happen," James told Michael.

"I knew he was right and I tried to change," Michael said. "I concentrated more on my schoolwork. I had a goal and I knew I had to work hard to reach it."

"Education was always a very strong priority with the Jordans," Kenneth McLaurin says. "Michael was a very strong academic student."

"My favorite subjects," Michael says, "were math and geography."

Janice Hardy taught math at Laney. She remembers Michael as "a nice, polite kid. I never heard him say an unkind word about anybody and he was well-liked by the students and by teachers, too."

"The first year I had him in geometry for two months. Then the class was split, so he chose to leave. He was afraid of me because he'd heard I was a tough teacher. But I had him the second year in algebra, too. In his senior year, I taught him trigonometry and advanced algebra. We eventually became good friends. He was an average student in math, but whenever he had trouble he always came for help after school."

"Mike could be a joker, too." David Bridgers adds. "He'd cut up in class and loved to see people laugh. But when it came to the books, he was a serious student."

Michael was a popular and outgoing student. He played the trumpet in the band for a while. He was a member of the Spanish Club, the Pep Club, and a homeroom monitor. He made friends easily and mixed with a variety of crowds, ranging from the athletes to members of the student government. "Everybody knew Mike," says David Bridgers.

Like many teenagers, however, Michael could be insecure and unsure of himself. Although his yearbook picture shows a cheerful young man with a winning smile, Michael thought he was "goony looking." His friends would tease him about his ears sticking out and his close-cropped "little boy haircut."

"A lot of guys picked on me and they would do it in front of the girls," he recalled. "They would joke about my haircut, and the way I played with my tongue out, and just different things. And the girls would laugh at that. Right then I was dead. I couldn't get a date with anybody. I always thought I would end up a bachelor, that no one would marry me."

Michael thought he would end up doing all his own sewing and cooking, and would have to run a household on his own.

"So I took home economics," Michael remembered. "I made a shirt; I can hem, cut out patterns, and do all that stuff." Michael also baked bread and cakes and brought them home. The family loved them and couldn't believe that Michael had made them.

During the summer between tenth and eleventh grades, Michael grew four inches. He was now six feet three inches and eager to claim a spot on the varsity basketball team. The four inches he'd grown made a big difference in his game and so did the constant practice he'd been getting. Michael would practice from five o'clock to seven in the evening with the junior varsity, taking part not only in their scrimmages, but also their drills and wind sprints. At seven o'clock, the varsity team began their practice and Michael was out there with them until nine.

"Other kids had just as much talent as he did," said Fred Lynch, "but they didn't want to pay dues the way Michael did."

Michael made the varsity team easily and was the hero of the holiday championship tournament. New Hanover High School was Laney's archrival and the game was a close battle until the final minutes. New Hanover had a slim lead when Michael went on a scoring spree. He drove, he dunked, he hit lay-ups, and banked shots off the backboard. New Hanover kept fighting back, and the score was tied as the clock ticked off the final seconds. One of the Laney players tossed a pass to Michael who let go a high hanging jump shot. The ball sailed through the net just as the buzzer sounded. Laney won, and Michael had scored all of his team's final 15 points. It was the beginning of a Jordan tradition of game-winning, fourth-quarter fireworks. The tradition continued through Michael's college and professional career.

3
A Turning Point

Although Michael was a star for Laney, he still wasn't considered anywhere near one of the top high school players in the country. Following the 1980 season, a publication for college scouts listed the top 300 prospects from all over America. Michael was not even mentioned.

However, in North Carolina, Michael, still a junior, was beginning to attract attention. Mike Brown, a graduate of the University of North Carolina (UNC) who worked in the Wilmington school system, told Dean Smith, UNC's coach, that he should check out the skinny kid from Laney High.

Smith's visit to Laney made Michael nervous. The UNC Tar Heels are a Division I team. The college teams in Division I are the best in the country. They attract the top high school players, and the Division I teams who play in the NCAA (National Collegiate Athletic Association) tournament each year are closely watched by pro scouts.

"I never thought I'd be able to play in Division

I," Michael admitted. "No one from my high school ever had."

Michael wanted to meet Smith, but his shyness got the better of him. After the game, Michael avoided Smith's gaze and stood dribbling a ball in a corner of the gym.

In the summer following his junior year, Michael got to know Dean Smith better when he attended the coach's basketball camp at UNC at Chapel Hill. At the camp, Michael met a young man from Asheville named Buzz Peterson. Buzz was considered a top college prospect. Michael and Buzz were roommates at the camp and became good friends.

"Mike was a real nice guy, very friendly and always joking around. He was very upbeat. We hit it off right from the start. He wasn't a very polished basketball player at the time, but he was a good athlete. He really could jump. You could throw an alley-oop pass to him and he could dunk it," Buzz remembered.

Later that summer, Michael and Buzz attended Howie Garfinkel's Five-Star Camp in Pittsburgh, Pennsylvania. The camp was a training ground for up-and-coming high school players. Many of the teenagers who attended would end up recruited by college scouts. Every player at the camp had to be invited to attend. Michael hadn't received an actual invitation to the camp. He wasn't regarded as enough of a top prospect to merit one. However, Roy Williams, one of Dean Smith's assistants, and Laney's varsity coach, Clifton Herring, wrote letters of recommendation and Michael was asked to come to the camp. To help pay his expenses, Michael got a job at the camp as a waiter. Although Michael had doubts he was good enough to go, he was elated.

"I felt like someone had tapped me on the shoulder with a magic wand," Michael said.

"Michael was an unknown when he came to the camp," Buzz notes. "He had been playing football, basketball, and baseball. Now he was concentrating on one sport and you could see he was getting better and better all the time."

If Michael was regarded as a questionable talent when he arrived at the camp, he was soon regarded as a hot prospect. What impressed people most was Michael's leaping ability when he pulled down rebounds, took a jump shot, or dunked.

"It was like there was no defender. It was like he was playing a different game," said camp official Tom Konchalski.

Michael was named Most Valuable Player and won ten trophies for scoring, defense, and other individual achievements. More important, the experience gave Michael more confidence in himself and his skills. "It was the turning point of my life," Michael often says.

When Michael returned to Laney in the fall, he was two inches taller. The previous year, his father had walked into Michael's room and had seen him hanging on his chin-up bar for minutes at a time. When James asked his son what he was doing, Michael replied that he was trying to stretch himself and become taller. James had just laughed. Michael was now six feet five inches. His shoulders had also become wider and his legs had grown more muscular.

Michael used his height and strength to power the Laney team over its opponents in his senior year. He averaged 23 points per game and broke all of the school's scoring records.

Even in those days, Michael attracted sellout crowds. "Michael was a star," Kenneth McLaurin remembers. "In his senior year, the varsity basketball games started at seven-thirty. By five o'clock, the gym would be packed."

At the end of the season, Laney High won its first conference championship. Michael finished second in the voting for the North Carolina High School Player of the Year, behind Buzz Peterson.

Michael now looked ahead to college. He believed he could play Division I ball, so he wrote to UCLA, whose team had won countless championships and produced basketball greats like Kareem Abdul-Jabbar. Michael never got an answer from the school. Michael also was interested in the University of Virginia where seven-foot-four-inch center Ralph Sampson was making headlines. Even though he hadn't been a University of North Carolina (UNC) fan, he also considered going to school in Chapel Hill. He and Buzz had talked about going to UNC together and becoming roommates.

The UNC Tar Heels were a top-ranked team, thanks to Dean Smith's coaching. Michael also admired Walter Davis, whose picture-perfect jump shot had taken the Tar Heels to the 1977 NCAA finals. The Jordans visited the UNC campus, and

Michael liked what he saw. The campus was quiet and friendly. Students lounged on the lawn, studying under the shade of the tall trees that surrounded the stately brick buildings.

As he toured the campus, Michael saw a bunch of students organizing a pickup game of basketball. Unable to resist a game, Michael introduced himself and told them he was considering attending UNC. He asked if he could join them. Michael proceeded to astound the students with a series of dunks and reverse lay-ups. By the time the game was over, there were students watching the game from the windows of the nearby dormitories.

Dean Smith also impressed the Jordans. He was soft-spoken and didn't make outrageous promises or offers. He stressed academics as well as athletics and wanted only well-rounded students on his team. Smith told Michael his B average would qualify for a scholarship. Michael, he said, would make a great addition to the team, but only if he kept his grades up. James and Deloris were relieved to hear that and they encouraged Michael to think seriously about attending UNC.

Of all the college coaches who tried to recruit Michael, Dean Smith was the only one who didn't promise Michael a starting spot on his team. That didn't bother Michael. He took it as a challenge.

Michael returned to Laney more determined than ever to improve his game. He awoke every morning at dawn, left the house at 6:00 A.M., and drove to the high school with varsity coach Clifton Herring. He practiced before school, after school, and often into the evening. Herring worked with him, offering pointers and basic playing tips. Michael always believed those senior-year sessions gave him a head start over many other players.

"When I was young, I had to learn the fundamentals of basketball," Michael explained many years later. "You can have all the physical ability in the world but you still have to know the fundamentals."

Not everyone thought Michael should attend UNC. Some of his friends thought he should go to a smaller Division III school where he would get more playing time.

"People back in his hometown were telling him that he'd never get to play and that he'd sit on the bench at North Carolina," Buzz confirms. "He wanted to go there to prove everyone wrong. He was a very determined person and he had a lot of heart."

It was rare for a freshman to make the varsity team at UNC. It was even rarer for one to break into the starting lineup. A few of Michael's friends wisecracked that if he went to UNC he'd have a great seat for every game — on the bench.

"Some people thought I'd never make a college basketball team, let alone the pros," Michael recalls. Some of his more skeptical friends predicted he'd end up back in Wilmington four years later, pumping gas. Others, like Laney principal Kenneth McLaurin, suggested a less-risky career path.

"My high school principal advised me to go to the Air Force Academy so that after college I would have a job." Michael remembered.

Math teacher Janice Hardy suggested another

career alternative. "I told Michael he should major in math, because that was where the money was," she says with a hearty laugh.

Michael made up his mind to go to UNC. His sister Roslyn would be going with him. She had skipped a grade and had been accepted at Chapel Hill, too. The Jordans were glad that Michael would have a family member close by.

Michael graduated from Laney High School in June of 1981. He had learned a lot in school. However, as he would always do, he credited his parents with teaching him life's most important lessons, lessons that would help him avoid the pitfalls that could tempt a young man in big-time college sports.

"My parents warned me about the traps, the drugs, the streets that could catch you if you were careless," Michael says. "I may have been lazy, but I wasn't careless."

"I had great parental guidance when I was young," Michael adds. "They taught me, from day one, right from wrong. And you know, dealing with drugs and alcohol, that's wrong. I know that what I do has to be right. I could have easily had parents who didn't care and let me hang out late nights with the wrong crowd," Michael declares. "I wasn't brought up that way and it was easy for me to distinguish the environment I wanted to be in from the environment I didn't want to be in."

"The Jordans had that commitment and discipline. They were a very strong family unit," Kenneth McLaurin confirms. "Michael had a very stable home environment."

Few people had any idea that Michael was destined to be a basketball superstar. "We never thought he would take the NBA by storm like he did," Kenneth McLaurin says. "I remember one day in his senior year I was sitting in my office and the door was open and Michael came in in a playful, joking mood. I said to Michael, 'I'm going to have the yearbook staff pick a glossy black-and-white photo of you because if you ever amount to anything, I'm going to sell it,'" the principal said with a laugh. "Michael just laughed."

Underneath Michael's picture in the 1981 Laney yearbook is the following inscription: "Laney only hopes that you expand your talents to make others as proud of you as Laney has been."

Michael's talents would not only expand, but were about to explode and bring him national exposure beyond his wildest dreams.

4
Learning the Game

Michael quickly discovered that college ball was far different from the basic plays he had learned at Laney. Coach Smith stressed teamwork, defense, and a tightly controlled offensive system called the Four Corners. Players would form a box-like pattern around the basket and work the ball around from the wings to the corners until someone had a clear shot. The system relied on pinpoint passing and the scoring talents of all the players, not just one shooting star.

The system had made the Tar Heels a top-ranked team. In the 21 years Smith had coached the team, the Tar Heels had made it to the NCAA finals five times, and the title game twice, but they had never won the NCAA championship. One sportswriter dubbed him, "the greatest coach to never win a championship."

Championships were the last thing on Michael's mind as he settled into college life. He signed up for classes in geography, math, English, and other subjects.

Since Michael had won a basketball scholarship, he did not have to take a job to help pay his expenses. Between classes and practice, he hardly had time for either a job or socializing. Buzz Peterson had decided to attend UNC, and he and Michael rented an apartment together in Chapel Hill. Even though they both played guard, the two young men became best friends rather than rivals.

Michael's Laney High classmates had been right about one thing. Freshmen didn't have a terrific track record making Dean Smith's starting lineup. Only seven freshmen had ever made the team. Just three, including UNC's then current star and future Los Angeles Laker, James Worthy, had broken into the starting five. Michael looked with awe at teammates like Worthy, Al Wood, Jimmy Black, Sam Perkins, and the seven-foot Geoff Crompton.

"When I came here I thought everybody was a superstar," Michael told a local reporter later in the season. "I thought I would be low man."

Michael made both the team *and* the starting lineup. The team's practice sessions were filled with all kinds of drills, from passing and dribbling exercises to defensive and shooting ones. Freshman players, no matter how talented, still had to undergo a sort of hazing. The upperclassmen selected Michael to carry the heavy film projector on the team's first road trip. Still, Michael couldn't help feeling thrilled as the Tar Heels won ten straight games.

A big crowd turned out at UNC's Carmichael Arena for the 1981–82 home opener against the University of Tulsa. The UNC students got a good introduction to Michael. The 19-year-old freshman scored 22 points in 22 minutes and stole the ball several times as the Tar Heels defeated Tulsa 78–70.

Michael played well for most of the season, but in the last two weeks, he slumped. To make matters worse, he came down with a terrible sore throat on the eve of the Atlantic Coast Conference tournament. Doctors thought he might have to go into the hospital to have his tonsils removed. The night before the first-round game against Georgia Tech, however, the team doctor decided the operation wasn't needed. Michael scored 18 points as the Tar Heels defeated Georgia 55–39. After the regular season ended, Michael was named the ACC Rookie of the Year.

The Tar Heels' record was good enough to qualify them for the 1982 NCAA tournament. They survived the grueling playoffs and made it to the championship game. Their opponent was the Georgetown Hoyas, a formidable team whose freshman center was future New York Knicks' star Patrick Ewing. The seven-foot tall Ewing was one of the most intimidating shot blockers in college basketball. Opposing teams had nicknamed him "The Hoya Destroyer." Eric "Sleepy" Floyd, despite his nickname, was another Hoya threat who had scored 2,300 points in his college career.

More than 61,000 fans, including James, Deloris, and James Ronald Jordan, jammed the New

Orleans Superdome for the game. All the Tar Heels knew that the game meant a lot to Dean Smith. In 1977, the Tar Heels had faced Marquette in the championship game and lost. In the season before Michael arrived at UNC, the Tar Heels were considered the favorite to win the NCAA crown. That team didn't even get past the regional finals. Some writers blamed the team's defeat on Smith's insistence on using his tightly controlled Four Corners offense.

The game began slowly, and it wasn't until eight minutes into the match that James Worthy scored the Tar Heels' first basket. Despite Ewing's height advantage, Michael held his own under the boards, pulling down nine rebounds, more than any other UNC player. The Tar Heels battled back, and with three minutes remaining in the game, they had gained a one-point lead, 59–58. Moments later, Michael drove past Ewing and lofted a high arcing shot over his outstretched arms. The ball fell through the net, putting the Tar Heels ahead by three, 61–58. Ewing retaliated with a fall-away jumper to pull within one, 61–60. The Tar Heels searched for a shot, but the Hoyas played tough defense, jamming up the center lane, and forcing them to the outside.

A minute later, Ewing grabbed the rebound off a missed shot and fired the ball to Eric Floyd. Floyd hit a 12-foot jumper, and the Hoyas were ahead 62–61 with 32 seconds to go. The Tar Heels called time-out.

Dean Smith surveyed his team. James Worthy, who had scored 28 points, was drawing most of the attention from the Hoyas' defense. Sam Perkins, too, was being covered tightly. Michael was the third-leading scorer on the team, but he was getting open more than the other players. Coach Smith told his team to get the ball to Michael for a shot. As the Tar Heels headed back on court, the coach muttered "Make it, Michael."

UNC's Jimmy Black spotted Michael wide open near the right baseline and he fired a bounce pass to him. There were just 16 seconds left. Realizing they'd made a mistake, the Hoyas rushed toward Michael, hoping to shake his concentration.

"I thought Michael wasn't going to take the shot because there was so much pressure on him. I thought he'd go back inside to James Worthy," Buzz Peterson remembers. "But he was wide open and he took the shot."

In the third row, James Jordan closed his eyes. He couldn't watch. A split second later, when the Superdome erupted in deafening cheers, James knew the shot had gone in. The Tar Heels were ahead 63–62.

The Hoyas got the ball again. Eric Floyd broke free from his defender, and Fred Brown threw a pass in his direction. James Worthy, however, stepped between Brown and Floyd and stole the pass. Moments later the final buzzer sounded.

"It's over!" Michael shouted. He rushed over to hug Jimmy Black and Dean Smith. Many of the players were crying with joy. It was James Worthy's last college game. He was set to join the Lakers the following year, and Michael's shot had given him the best going-away present a college player could ask for. For Coach Smith, years of disappointment were washed away. The Four Corners system had worked, and Smith and his staff felt vindicated.

In the locker room, James Jordan hugged his son. "I couldn't look," James told a reporter. "I ducked my head and asked Ronald if it went in. Michael won some games in the last second in high school, but this is a far cry from high school."

After the game, Michael and Buzz went for a walk down Bourbon Street in New Orleans. Michael was quiet for a few minutes, then he turned to Buzz and said, "That was a pretty big shot."

"You're doggone right it was," Buzz answered. "And in about ten years, it will be even bigger," Buzz predicted.

"I'm glad I went ahead and shot the ball when I caught it," Michael confided. "Because if I'd have hesitated, I never would have made it."

Michael's game-winning jumper would become a college basketball legend. The shot also changed his life and gave him his first taste of national exposure.

"A lot of people didn't know I existed until I got it," Michael says. "When I hit that shot, it was like I was different. I won a national championship. I think people started to recognize my talents more, and I started getting more publicity. I think that shot really put me on the map."

"The Shot," as it became known, also gave Michael's self-confidence a boost.

"When he hit 'The Shot,'" Buzz Peterson remembers, "he picked up a lot of confidence. He didn't have all the moves he has now, but you could see him improving every day."

Michael was honored with a Michael Jordan Day on his return to Wilmington. On the UNC campus, he was suddenly a celebrity. A photo of "The Shot" would adorn the cover of the new edition of the Chapel Hill phone book. He was besieged by reporters for interviews, and on campus perfect strangers rushed up to ask for autographs.

"At first I enjoyed the public recognition," Michael admitted. "Three years ago I never dreamed that a kid would ask me for an autograph. But at times the recognition can be worrisome, too. When I'm in a restaurant, for instance, it's embarrassing. Basketball seems to follow me the whole day."

Despite his newfound fame, Michael was still somewhat shy. "He was a big man on campus," Buzz remembers, "but he wouldn't go out of his way to introduce himself to girls. He wouldn't do that at all. He would wait until they came up to him. He didn't really like large groups of people either. He was happy with a small group of friends."

Michael avoided the parties and late-night carousing some of his teammates indulged in. He preferred to hang out with Buzz at the student center playing videogames, shooting pool, and playing Ping-Pong. Buzz soon found out that Michael could be just as competitive off the court as he was on.

"We were playing Monopoly one night," Buzz remembers, "and he was losing really bad. Finally he just gave up and said, 'I've lost,' and he threw the board and money all over. He really wasn't serious. It was all in fun, but I never let him forget about that — being such a bad sport.

"If you were playing cards or shooting pool, he hated to lose. Michael probably got that from growing up with two older brothers who would pick on him and beat him up. He just hated losing. He was the most competitive person I'd ever been around," Buzz declares.

Michael himself agrees with that. "I am probably the most competitive person in the world. I compete at everything," he says.

Michael has a simple explanation for this competitive streak. "Being competitive is really a way to constantly challenge myself, and I like to challenge myself in every aspect of my life. I believe that there is always room for improvement."

Buzz also saw another side of Michael. "Michael was the kind of guy who looked after you. I remember one time I left for a weekend to go to Asheville where my parents live. I had sweaters and clothes scattered everywhere. I got back and Mike had it all piled up neatly all in the right spots," Buzz said. "He was the kind of person you'd want to have as a close friend."

Michael spent most of the summer of his freshman year playing pickup games at Woollen Gym on the UNC campus. Coach Smith believed Michael had tremendous potential, but thought his game had been inconsistent. He and Michael studied game films from his freshman season and pinpointed areas for improvement. Michael needed to work on his outside shooting, his defensive game, and his ball-handling skills. When Michael began dribbling the ball, his powerful legs allowed him to get a very fast start. In the pros, Michael would use this speed to drive past defensive players and beat them to the basket. As a college freshman, however, his speed sometimes resulted in turnovers. Michael was so quick that he occasionally left the ball behind when he began his dribble.

With James Worthy gone, Michael and Sam Perkins became the team leaders. Michael drove himself hard and pushed the other players, even in practice. His competitiveness was evident, and he delighted in dunking on his teammates again and again.

"We'd do a lot of one-on-one drills," recalls Buzz Peterson. "One on one, Michael was, and still is, very tough to handle because of his quick first step. It was like he had oil on him. He'd slide right around you and dunk on you. He got to a point in his sophomore year when his confidence was really rolling and he'd tease the guys. He dunked on everybody. Then he'd get in the locker room and write on the blackboard, 'Dunked twice on Kenny Smith, Buzz Peterson — twice.' That's the type of person he was. He was joking about it, having a lot of fun. He was that way off the court, too.

"A lot of guys who didn't know him had a hard time understanding him because Michael was a very confident person. He might tell you that he was going to dunk on someone twice in a game. People would laugh, but Michael would do it. He always backed up his words. Once Michael's team-mates found that out, they just let it go by. But if someone came off the street and Michael did that, they said he was real cocky. But it takes a bit of cockiness to be a great player. When you step onto the court, you've got to say, 'I'm the best player out there.' Michael has always been that type of player and that's what he's always said. He expects to be the best player and he's got to do that every night."

5
Big Man on Campus

No one would have guessed that the Tar Heels were the defending NCAA champions from their first three games in Michael's sophomore year. The team opened the 1982–83 season with losses to St. John's University, the University of Missouri, and Tulane University. The team finally won its first game as Michael's developing defensive skills helped sink Syracuse. He blocked shots and made several key steals. Against the University of Maryland, Michael ensured a Tar Heels' victory by blocking a shot in the final seconds.

He was offensive dynamite, too. He played 23 minutes and scored 32 points in a 103–82 blowout against the powerful Duke University Blue Devils. Taking on Georgia Tech, Michael showed his sharpshooting skills with a deadly run of seven 3-pointers. Michael's 39 points — his season high — was more than half of his team's point total as the Tar Heels won 72–65.

The Tar Heels met the University of Virginia

Cavaliers on a chilly night in February. The Cavaliers were a tough team and their seven-foot-four-inch center, Ralph Sampson, was one of the most feared shot blockers in college ball.

The Cavaliers had a 16-point lead with eight minutes to go. The Tar Heels fought back and closed the gap to 63–60 with a minute left. Leaping over Sampson, Michael scored to bring the Tar Heels within one.

"Michael hit that shot," Buzz Peterson remembers, "then just stripped the ball from Rick Carlisle right in the middle of the court. Then he went down and dunked it, and we took a one-point lead. Virginia came down and shot, but missed. Michael grabbed the rebound over Ralph Sampson and the game ended. What he did in less than a minute was an unbelievable performance."

Michael's late-game heroics won him increased attention from newspapers all over the state. The *Durham Sun* called him, "the best all-around player in college basketball."

When Duke returned to UNC for a rematch, Michael's 32 points sealed a Tar Heels' victory. But the team lost the Atlantic Coast Conference tournament to their rival North Carolina State, then were eliminated by Georgia in the NCAA playoffs.

The next day, Michael was back in Woollen Gym practicing and working out. "The season didn't end quite like I wanted it, but I enjoyed it anyway. I love playing and I just wanted to start working for this year," he said.

Michael had averaged 20 points and 5.5 rebounds per game. His 78 steals was the second-best total in UNC history. His two-season point total of 1,100 was a Tar Heels' record.

The Sporting News named Michael College Player of the Year, saying, "He soars through the air, he rebounds, he scores, he guards two men at once. He vacuums up loose balls. He makes steals. Most important, he makes late plays that win games. Call it what you may, court sense or court presence. He has it."

The awards that meant most to Michael, however, were two of the team awards he won at the end of the season. Every year, Dean Smith and his coaching staff gave out offensive and defensive awards. In his freshman year, Michael hadn't won any. This time he won twelve, including two for defensive play. The defensive awards pleased Michael most.

The summer following his sophomore year, Michael and a team of college all-stars traveled to Caracas, Venezuela, to take part in the Pan Am Games. Michael was the team's leading scorer and the U.S. squad won a gold medal.

The trip to South America made a big impression on Michael. It gave him a glimpse of a culture far different than any he had seen before. He was excited to see different people and places, and the trip was an eye-opening experience.

Later that summer, the Tar Heels toured Greece and played a series of international exhibition games. Coach Smith arranged for a UNC history professor to accompany the team. The professor gave the players lectures on Greek history and culture as they traveled and visited the magnificent monuments and ruins.

"At first I didn't want to go because of all the travel," Michael admitted. "But then I enjoyed it. I enjoyed seeing history and what we've been through to get to this point, and to feel what it's like to be one of billions of people who have lived. That can be helpful," Michael added, "for those who have big heads."

When Michael returned to Chapel Hill for his junior year, he practiced every day and began a weight training program that would add twelve pounds of muscle to his upper body and legs. He grew another inch and now stood six-foot-six-inches and weighed 190 pounds. Michael was fast, too. He could run the 40-yard dash in just 4.3 seconds.

Michael was also a solid student. "Mike didn't take the easy road that some athletes do," David Bridgers recalls. "He didn't take a lot of physical education courses. He was busy taking courses in computer science."

"Mike was a good student," Buzz Peterson confirms. "He wasn't a top student, but he was always very conscientious with his work."

As a junior, Michael had to choose a major in his studies. His recent travels had broadened his horizons and shown him people and places far different from any he'd seen in North Carolina. He decided to major in geography.

Dean Smith also made a small but important contribution to Michael's education. After his game-winning shot against Georgetown, Michael had found himself in the spotlight more and more. Smith sensed that someday Michael would face even more media attention, so he encouraged Michael to take a public-speaking course.

On the court and on campus, Michael felt tremendous pressure. Everyone expected the 20-year-old to lead the Tar Heels to another NCAA title. In the face of such high hopes, Michael's game suffered. In the first few games of the season, it became obvious to Coach Smith that Michael was not playing up to his usual standards.

Michael could see it, too. He and Coach Smith studied films from his sophomore year, then compared them with the ones from the 1983–84 season. "It was like a totally different person," Michael noted. "You could see exactly what success had done to me. From that point on I was able to deal with it."

The Tar Heels finished the season with 28 wins and 3 losses. Michael was the top scorer in the Atlantic Coast Conference with a 19.5 point average. Dean Smith's Four Corners had emphasized a team scoring effort, rather than reliance on the talents of a single shooter. As a result, people would later joke when Michael was a high-scoring pro that the only person to consistently hold Michael to less than 20 points was Dean Smith!

Smith also stressed the basics: teamwork, defense, and passing. There was a role for good shooters, but not show-offs. According to Buzz Peterson and others, Coach Smith didn't hold Michael back at all. The opposite was true, according to Buzz. "Mike really learned a lot from Dean Smith's program," he says.

David Bridgers went to many games at Chapel Hill during Michael's college years. He could see that Michael's skills had grown since high school. "Mike did a smart thing by going to Chapel Hill with Dean Smith. He could have gone to the University of Maryland and showboated a little bit, like he does now in the pros. He let Dean Smith teach him the values of the game. Mike really matured when he was there."

He and Sam Perkins led the Tar Heels to the ACC championship. With players like Kenny Smith and Brad Daugherty, both of whom would go on to be NBA players, UNC was expected to win the NCAA crown once again. The Tar Heels met Indiana in the semifinals. The Indiana Hoosiers, coached by the fiery Bobby Knight, beat the Tar Heels 72–68 as Michael got into foul trouble and had to leave the game. It was a tremendous disappointment for Michael and his teammates.

In that off-season, Michael discovered golf.

"In our junior year, Michael and I had a couple of classes with Jack Nicklaus, Jr., and a guy named Davis Love III, who's now on the Pro Golfers Association tour," Buzz Peterson remembers. "After we lost to Indiana we had nothing to do after classes so Davis said, 'Come on out and hit some golf balls.' We played nine holes that day. The next day we played eighteen. Soon we were doing it every day. Michael struggled with golf at first. When we first started playing I could beat him, no problem. Michael was just as competitive when he played golf, but he used to lose all the time."

Michael discovered that the golf course was a place where he could escape not only fans and reporters, but also the pressures of basketball. It was the start of what would become Michael's love affair with the sport.

"I never thought Michael would fall in love with golf when we first started playing," Buzz said. "I thought it might become a hobby for him, but he went head over heels for the game."

Pro basketball scouts were now beginning to look at Michael as a hot prospect. He had the potential, some said, to join the ranks of the NBA's greatest guards, players like Jerry West, and Oscar "The Big O" Robertson. Michael's only weakness, according to scouting reports, was his outside shot.

Michael was beginning to think that he needed more of a challenge than college ball offered. His former teammate, James Worthy, had left UNC as a junior to go pro. Worthy was now a member of the Los Angeles Lakers and had already played in an NBA championship. Michael began to think seriously about leaving school to go pro. He was torn between finishing college and declaring himself eligible for the NBA draft in June.

"Michael knew he could be a top pro player. He never told me that, but I knew he was thinking that," Buzz Peterson says.

But Michael liked the friendly environment at Chapel Hill and he enjoyed the respect and admiration he received from his coaches and classmates. The idea of leaving school without a degree also troubled Michael. It worried his mother, too. Deloris was against Michael leaving school early. If a pro career didn't work out, Michael would be left with no skills and no job when his playing days ended. She told him, "No matter where you go and how much money you make, education will always win out. They can take your clothes, they can take your shoes, but they can't take away what's in your head."

Dean Smith and James Jordan thought Michael was ready for the pros. Many other less-talented players had not only survived the pros but thrived in them.

Michael finally won Deloris's approval when he promised to return to UNC the next two summers and get his degree.

Some UNC fans were not convinced. They said Michael owed it to the school to play his senior year and lead the Tar Heels to a national title again. Michael bristled when he heard that. "I don't owe the fans or alumni another year at this university," he said. "I have to do what's best for me. If I owe anyone, it's my parents who have put up with me for 20 years."

A press conference was scheduled for the morning of May 4 on the Chapel Hill campus. The evening before, Michael had last-minute doubts.

"We went out to eat at a Japanese restaurant, and he had no idea what he was going to do," Buzz says.

He and Buzz talked late into the night, and when Michael went to bed, he still was not 100 percent sure of what he would do.

Michael overslept the next morning and nearly was late for the press conference. He got dressed quickly, pulling on a yellow shirt and a pair of dark pants.

"When he left the room that morning to go to the press conference, I said, 'What are you going to do?' " Buzz remembers. "He said, 'Buzz, I don't really know.' "

When he arrived at the press conference it was packed with reporters and TV crews. Michael sat down in front of a microphone. With his parents and Dean Smith at his side, Michael announced he was leaving UNC to play pro ball.

"I'll tell you the truth," Michael said after a reporter asked him when he had made the decision. "I just decided half an hour ago. I was 50–50. I talked to Coach this morning. He helped me. My parents helped me. Everything looks bright for me. It's time for me to move on."

Michael described his time at UNC as "the best years of my life." He praised Dean Smith, saying, "Coach Smith challenged us on the court, but also encouraged us in the classroom."

Smith would remain a lifelong friend and Michael would return to Chapel Hill many times in his pro career to visit his former coach. In 1986, Michael and the Chicago Bulls came to Carmichael Arena at UNC to play a preseason game. Dean Smith took Michael aside after the game and led him to the team's supply room. He pulled out a box of blue UNC basketball shorts and handed it to Michael as a good luck gift. Michael began wearing the shorts under his Bulls' uniform and it has been a Jordan ritual ever since.

"I never go anywhere without my Carolina blues," he now says.

Michael picked up another habit at UNC that he would carry into the pros. When a knee injury sidelined Buzz Peterson in his sophomore year, Michael had begun wearing a black sweatband on his arm as if to mourn the loss of his teammate. Michael still wears one, although he alternates between black and white depending on whether the Bulls are home or away.

Michael left behind more than a legend at UNC. He left his number 23 UNC jersey which the university retired. It now hangs on a wall at Chapel Hill.

Many factors had made Michael a success at UNC. While teammates and coaches played crucial roles in his development both as a person and an athlete, one important quality, Michael believes, came from within.

"The one thing I developed on my own was my determination. I acquired that when I was small," he said.

That determination would soon turn him into a rookie sensation in the NBA, not to mention win him an Olympic gold medal.

6
Here Comes Mr. Jordan

In June of 1984, representatives from twenty-three NBA teams gathered in a New York hotel ballroom to conduct the annual college draft. Each team got the chance to select from the most talented college players, the order largely determined by the previous season's standings. The teams with the worst records usually got the first picks, although teams could trade away veteran players to obtain a higher pick. In the 1984 draft, it seemed as though everyone was looking for a big man.

The Houston Rockets had the first pick. They chose Hakeem Olajuwon, a six-foot-ten-inch Nigerian-born player who had scored 1,332 points in three seasons at the University of Houston. The Portland Trail Blazers had the second pick. They selected seven-foot-one-inch Sam Bowie, who played both forward and center.

"Michael wanted to be one of the first five picks," Buzz Peterson remembers. "The team he really liked most was Philadelphia. He wanted to play for the 76ers, but he knew he had to go with the team that picked him."

The Chicago Bulls had the third pick. The previous year, the Bulls had the second-worst record in the Eastern Conference. Only one team had a lower winning percentage. In the previous ten years, the Bulls had had just three winning seasons. They were hoping to use their selection to help turn the team into a winner.

"The Chicago Bulls," the announcer called out, "pick Michael Jordan of the University of North Carolina." A group of fans in the back of the room cheered loudly and the Bulls' representatives at the team table gave the thumbs-up sign.

Quite a few people said at the time that the Rockets and the Trail Blazers had made a big mistake.

George Raveling, assistant coach of the U.S. Olympic basketball team predicted, "In two or three years, there will be a major controversy in the NBA. It will be about how Michael Jordan was allowed to be drafted only third instead of first or second."

Even the Bulls didn't realize how lucky they were to have chosen Michael. The Bulls also thought they needed a big center to turn the team into a contender.

"Olajuwon was the big prize," Bulls' general manager Rod Thorn conceded after the draft. Of Michael, he said, "We wished he was seven feet tall but he isn't. There just wasn't a center available."

The Bulls knew Michael was a great player. They just didn't think that the six-foot-six-inch guard could turn the Bulls around. It seemed too big a job for one player. The team hoped Michael would score 17 to 19 points per game at best.

As one of the best college players that year, Michael was named co-captain of the 1984 U.S. Olympic basketball team. The games were scheduled for July in Los Angeles. "Competing in the Olympics," Michael said, "is a dream that I've had for a long time."

Michael's teammates included his one-time NCAA adversary Patrick Ewing, Chris Mullin, a sure-shooting junior from St. John's, and Sam Perkins, Michael's Tar Heels' teammate. Bobby Knight, the team's coach, had just six weeks to whip his team into shape. Knight had a reputation as one of the toughest coaches in college basketball. He demanded complete dedication from his players, and Michael impressed Knight early on with his skill and competitive nature.

To prepare the Olympians for the Summer Games, a series of exhibition games with an "all-star" NBA team was set up. The rotating roster of the NBA team included some genuine all-stars like Larry Bird, Magic Johnson, Isiah Thomas, and Kevin McHale, but others were average NBA players.

In Indianapolis, more than 60,000 flag-waving fans turned out at the airport to greet the college stars. Before the game, Michael got a chillier reception from Larry Bird. The 21-year-old experienced his first pro put-down from the Celtics' star.

During the pregame practice, one of the Olympians' basketballs rolled down to the other end of the court. Michael chased after it, but Larry Bird scooped it up. Michael reached out to take the ball, but Bird ignored him. Veteran players frequently gave NBA rookies a hard time, but Michael didn't expect Bird's next move. The NBA star kicked the ball over Michael's head and back to the other end of the court. Michael just shook his head and trotted downcourt.

Later Michael would tell his teammates, "Bird was showing me it was all business now, and I was beneath him. I didn't forget."

The Olympians took seven in a row from the pro players, and Michael was often the leading scorer. When the eighth game began in Milwaukee, the pros were eager for revenge. They had held just one practice session and were relying on strength rather than skill to counter the collegians. Michael and his teammates quickly found out that basketball could be a contact sport.

Elbows flew, and the pros set up screens that not only blocked the Olympians, but knocked them down in the process. The tone of the game was established early in the first quarter when Mickey Johnson of the Golden State Warriors knocked down Wayman Tisdale and Chris Mullin at the same time. Later Michael was knocked to the floor, too. The pros committed 30 fouls in the second half alone. Angered by the pros' cheap shots, the Olympians ran up a 22-point lead by the fourth quarter and won the game by a 94–78 margin. A sportswriter joked that if the Olympians had team colors, they would be red, white, black, and blue!

The collegians were more than ready for the Olympics. No country had dominated Olympic basketball like the United States had. Prior to the 1984 Games, American teams had won 69 of 70 games.

The Americans eliminated China, Canada, and Uruguay in rapid succession. The gold-medal game against Spain was scheduled for August 10 at the Forum in Inglewood. The Spanish team scored first, but the lead didn't last long. The United States team played with an intensity the Spaniards had never seen. The Americans hit 12 of their first 14 shots and took a 25–17 lead.

Spain's main offensive weapon was Fernando Romay, a six-foot-eleven-and-a-half-inch center. Romay kept his team in the game, and by the middle of the second half, Spain had narrowed the lead to just four points. Michael and his teammates turned on the defense and shut Romay down. Then they turned on the offense, and for every shot Spain missed, the Americans sunk one. Michael ended up with a team-high 20 points as the United States won the game 96–65, and the gold medal. The team had won all eight of its games. The average margin of victory had been 32.1 points, the second best in Olympic history.

Fernando Martin, one of Spain's best players, was awestruck by Michael's performance. His English was limited, but countless newspapers quoted him anyway when he said, "Michael Jordan? Jump, jump, jump. Very quick. Very fast, very, very good. Jump, jump, jump!"

The coach of the Spanish team, Antonio Diaz-Miguel, was more descriptive. "He's not human," the coach said. "He's a rubber man."

At a press conference, Michael displayed his gold medal to a crowd of reporters. Michael thanked the crowd and praised his teammates and coach Bobby Knight. He also thanked his parents. He turned to his mother who was standing next to him and took his gold medal and placed it around her neck. As Michael hugged her, tears of joy rolled down her cheeks.

If anyone still needed persuading that Michael had the right stuff to make it in the pros, his Olympic performance did the job convincingly. The Chicago Bulls were making the most of Michael's fame. The team began a "Here Comes Mr. Jordan" ad campaign that had Chicago fans anxiously awaiting Michael's arrival. And Michael would not disappoint them.

The Bulls' history, however, had been disappointing to the sports-crazy Chicago fans. The Bulls joined the NBA in 1966, and it wasn't until their fifth year that they had a winning season. In 1983–84, the season prior to Michael's arrival, the team had finished next to last in their division with a 27–55 record.

Chicago Bulls fans — the few that there were — were hoping Michael could end the team's losing streak. Fans hadn't exactly been flocking to buy Bulls' tickets. In the years before Michael Jordan joined the team, average attendance for home games hovered around 6,000 per game. On the road, the Bulls were even less of a draw.

Michael was a certified star, and his contract with the Bulls proved it. He signed for a salary of $4 million for five years, the best terms at that time for a first-year guard. But what was most interesting about Michael's contract with the Bulls was his "love of the game" clause. Most star players were forbidden by their teams from playing pickup games during the season. An injury in one of these games could cost a player his career and his team a lot of money. Michael couldn't resist a game and he insisted on being allowed to play whenever he wanted. The Bulls had no choice but to agree.

The Bulls' public relations department knew they had a good thing in Michael Jordan. Even before the season began, fans were flocking to Bulls' practice sessions at a Chicago high school to catch a glimpse of the rookie. Bulls fans who had given up their season tickets a year ago now were clamoring to get them back.

Michael not only had the potential to sell Bulls' tickets. Michael's management team had realized that he had the personality and image to sell other products as well. During his last days in college, Michael had hooked up with agent David Falk of ProServ, a sports management company. ProServ had started out representing tennis stars like Arthur Ashe and Stan Smith. Later it branched out to represent baseball and basketball players. ProServ had won for its clients all kinds of endorsement deals with makers of everything from sneakers to sporting goods to sportswear.

With Michael's clean-cut image and tremendous

personal charm, Falk realized that Michael could be a natural spokesman for a variety of products, and he arranged endorsement deals for Michael from companies like McDonald's, Coca-Cola, and Wilson, who made a Michael Jordan basketball.

Falk was also busy working out a $2.5 million endorsement deal with a sneaker company called Nike. Nike wanted Michael to endorse a new basketball sneaker they were in the process of designing. It was a red and white three-quarter height basketball sneaker that had air pockets in its sole. Michael, with his amazing ability to soar and score, was the perfect player to lend his name to the new venture. Falk and Nike had come up with the name Prime Time, but it sounded more like a TV show than a shoe. Falk wanted a name that would capture Michael's talents and personality. Suddenly he had a brainstorm. When Michael made his next visit to the ProServ offices, Falk announced the name was going to be "Air Jordan." Michael just laughed when he heard the name, but it stuck.

After his trip to the ProServ office, Michael returned to North Carolina where he paid a visit to Buzz Peterson.

"Hey, Buzz," Michael told his friend, "they're gonna name a shoe after me."

Buzz was used to Michael joking around and thought his friend was kidding.

Michael assured Buzz that it was no joke. "They're going to be called Air Jordans."

Buzz looked Michael right in the face. "Mike," he said. "You're a good basketball player, but you're not going to go into the NBA and turn everything around. You're not going to sell out every arena and you're not going to be better than Larry Bird or Magic Johnson. You're a good ballplayer, but not that good."

"You just wait and see," Michael responded with a smile.

"I had to eat my words," Buzz now admits with a laugh.

Within two years, Nike would sell more than $130 million worth of the shoes. Michael was described by *Business Week* magazine as "the greatest sneaker salesman the world has ever seen."

Despite his growing commercial success, Michael remained modest in his expectations. He knew that as a rookie he had a lot to learn from his more experienced teammates. Michael understood that there was no room for a one-man show. "It won't be the Michael Jordan show," he declared. "I'll just be a part of the team."

"I am very conscious of not being a prima donna. I wouldn't want that if I were a veteran and I try to put myself in our veterans' shoes," he explained.

In practices, Michael impressed his teammates with both his attitude and an amazing array of shots including what forward Steve Johnson described as "full speed slam dunks, forwards, backwards, and every which way."

In scrimmages, Bulls' coach Kevin Loughery found that the team with Michael nearly always won, even the second team. "No matter what I do with Michael, he wins," Loughery told a reporter.

Loughery believed that Michael had the talent

to be a superstar, but he thought the rookie needed to be pushed and challenged. Once during a practice, he nearly pushed Michael to his limit. Loughery divided the Bulls into red- and white-shirted teams and told them to begin a scrimmage game. The losing team, the coach said, would have to run extra laps after practice. Michael wasn't fond of running laps, and he liked losing even less. Michael and the red team took an early lead, 7–2, and needed four more baskets to win. Suddenly, Loughery blew his whistle for a time-out.

"Jordan," he shouted. "Switch with Higgins." Rod Higgins changed from white to red as Jordan fumed. Michael played to win and felt that Loughery was being unfair. Winning was meaningless if Loughery was going to make him change teams just because one side was losing. He felt like walking out of practice. Michael angrily pulled on a white jersey and pumped in seven shots in a row. With the white team leading, 10–8, Michael slammed a vicious dunk shot through the net to give his team the victory.

Michael was mad, but he later realized that Loughery wanted to push him and bring out the best in him. Loughery liked the way Michael played and saw his one-on-one skills as a potent weapon in the Bulls' offensive attack. Loughery would be fired at the end of the season, but Michael grew to respect him. Years later, Michael would describe Loughery as "the best coach I ever had. He pushed me to limits I didn't know I could reach."

Fueled by the Bulls' "Here Comes Mr. Jordan"

campaign, expectations were running high both in Chicago and in the NBA. Even Michael wondered if he could live up to the challenge. "I thought I would come out and be a flop because everyone was expecting so much," he said.

7
A Remarkable Rookie

As Michael got dressed before his first pro game, he felt a knot in his stomach. He was still nervous as he took the court and heard the cheers of the 13,913 fans who'd filled Chicago Stadium for the game against the Washington Bullets. Michael didn't have the greatest of games. He missed 11 of his 16 shots, but scored 16 points and got 7 assists. Michael had an eye-opening experience early in the game.

"During the first few minutes, I was knocked to the floor. It was then that I learned that basketball is a game of strength," Michael remembers.

Washington's Jeff Ruland had crashed into Michael and sent him sprawling on the floor. For thirty seconds, fans waited anxiously as Michael didn't get up. Finally, Michael picked himself up. The Bulls won 109–93.

"I'm just glad I could contribute," Michael told reporters after the game.

Throughout those early weeks, James and Deloris stayed close to Michael, attending games and helping him at home with shopping and other chores he was too busy to perform. The Jordans became a constant presence at Bulls' games.

"We wanted him to know that if you fall on your nose on the floor, there are people in the stands who still care about you. They'll love you anyway," Deloris said.

James and Deloris had little to worry about as far as Michael falling on his face.

In Michael's third pro game, he scored 37 points as the Bulls beat the Bucks 116–110. The Bucks double-teamed Michael, and he still was the Bulls' leading scorer. He was responsible for 20 of the Bulls' final 26 points.

Michael found that pro basketball was faster paced than college ball and the schedule suited him perfectly. "This is the most relaxed time of my career," Michael told *Sports Illustrated*. "The games come so quickly that if you have a bad one, you can put the past behind you and get ready for the present."

Michael didn't have many bad games to put behind him. On November 13, he scored 45 points against the San Antonio Spurs. Dean Smith had traveled to Chicago to see the game. "Michael's progress," he noted, "has been eerie."

When the Bulls met the Phoenix Suns two weeks later, Michael scored 22 points and the Suns' Michael Holton said, "All I saw were the bottoms of his shoes." Many other players would soon share that view.

The Bulls won five of their first seven games. It

was the best start the team had had since 1974. The Bulls had capable players like Orlando Woolridge, Dave Corzine, and Steve Johnson, but Michael was the spark that was firing up the team. Reporters dubbed the Bulls "Michael and the Jordanaires."

Michael was a big draw on the road, too. More than 20,000 fans showed up at New York's Madison Square Garden to watch the Bulls whip the Knicks 121–106. Michael was again the high scorer with 33 points. Jordan won the tough New York fans' respect when he stole the ball from Darrell Walker and broke toward the basket. Michael took the ball in one hand, and with a powerful tomahawk motion, slam dunked the ball through the net. The fans gave Michael a standing ovation.

"I expected a warm reception in Chicago," Michael said at the time. "But as for these crowds on the road, I can't express how good it feels to hear those cheers."

Michael was suddenly a celebrity. Michaelmania set in; everywhere he showed up, autograph seekers, flustered fans, reporters, and TV camera crews followed. The scenes reminded Michael's teammates of another Michael.

"Everywhere we go, it's like he's Michael and we're the Jacksons," Orlando Woolridge said.

When asked for an autograph, Michael would smile patiently and oblige the fans, no matter how many there were. Michael believed he owed the fans and basketball something in return for what basketball had given him.

"I'm not that special," Michael said modestly.

"Sure I play ball better than some and can do some things on a court. But why do people react like that around me, like I'm some kind of rock star or something?"

"I never thought it would be anything like this," he admitted. "There are a lot of stars in the NBA, Larry Bird, Dr. J, Magic Johnson, and Isiah Thomas." Michael found it unbelievable "for a rookie to come in and get this much publicity."

At home games, attendance at Chicago Stadium had doubled. Now more than 12,000 fans were coming to each game.

In November, the Bulls traveled to Los Angeles to play the Clippers. The crowd was packed with celebrities like Jack Nicholson, who had given up his Lakers' tickets to see the acclaimed Bulls' rookie. Michael gave the show-biz crowd a show of his own. For his first basket, Michael took on six-foot-eleven-inch Bill Walton. As Walton jumped to block the shot, Michael suddenly moved the ball from his right hand to his left, then back to his right, completely faking out the Clipper center as he scored. A few minutes later, Michael stung Norm Nixon with a back-to-the-basket, over-the-shoulder shot banked off the backboard.

The Clippers had a 100–98 lead with just over a minute to go in the game. Michael tied the game with an 18-foot jump shot, then stole a Clipper pass thirty seconds later. Michael raced down-court with Derek Smith of the Clippers right behind him. As Michael rose for the shot, Smith desperately grabbed him in a basketball version of a flying tackle. Michael still managed to get off the shot. It was good and it won the game.

"Incredible," said Derek Smith after the game. "Most people wouldn't have gotten the ball out of their hands."

Michael was asked at the time what his goals were for the season and beyond. "I hope I can say I did my best, achieved a lot, and won a couple of world championships. I'd also like to play in at least one All-Star game," Michael replied.

Michael was certainly playing like an All-Star. Two days after Christmas, Michael scored 45 points in a 112–108 victory over the Cleveland Cavaliers. A week later, he poured in 42 points against the Knicks in New York. On January 26, his 45 points helped crush the Atlanta Hawks 117–104.

Just before the NBA's All-Star weekend in February, the Boston Celtics, defending NBA champs, came into a sold-out Chicago Stadium for a match against the Bulls. Boston and Larry Bird beat the Bulls 110–106. Michael, however, won the Celtics' respect with a 41-point, 12-rebound game.

Larry Bird said he had never seen anyone like Michael. "He's phenomenal, one of a kind. I couldn't do what he did as a rookie. There was one drive tonight. He had the ball up in his right hand, then he took it down, then he brought it back up. I got a hand on it, fouled him, and he still scored. And all while he's in the air."

Chicago fans loved Michael's style, especially when he'd do one of his high-flying dunks. They began holding up cards like Olympic judges giving marks to a skater or gymnast. After Michael dunked, fans held up signs with perfect 10's, and occasional scores of 9.5.

Michael was such a favorite with fans, both at home and on the road, that he was voted onto the 1985 All-Star team. He was the first rookie starter since Isiah Thomas, who had done it three seasons earlier. Michael was so nervous at the prospect of playing in an All-Star Game that he said, "I probably won't remember how to play."

Michael showed up at the All-Star Game in Indianapolis in a flashy warm-up suit that Nike had asked him to wear. To some of the other All-Stars, who were following tradition by wearing their team uniforms, it seemed as if Michael was being boastful about his endorsements. Michael kept to himself, too nervous to rub shoulders with the best players in the league. To some of the All-Stars he seemed aloof and standoffish. To others he seemed cocky and brash. Several All-Stars decided it was time to teach the rookie a lesson and do it on national TV. During the All-Star Game, Isiah Thomas of the Detroit Pistons and some other players seemed to freeze Michael out. Michael didn't get his hands on the ball very much. When he was open for a shot, Michael's teammates appeared to be ignoring him. Michael, perhaps unnerved by the situation, did not play his best. In his 22 minutes in the game, he took nine shots and missed seven.

After the game, rumors swirled that Isiah Thomas had engineered the snub. The Pistons' star denied it. Sportswriters picked up on the rumors and wrote that the other All-Stars considered Michael to be a glory hound and arrogant. Later it was reported that Thomas and several other players had been seen at the airport laughing and talking about "teaching the rookie a lesson."

Michael was angry and embarrassed when he heard about the reports. "The whole thing makes me feel very small," he said. "The whole thing has hurt me, really hit me hard. I want to crawl into a hole and not come out. I don't want to be perceived as having an arrogant attitude," he explained. Then he added, "I won't forget what happened or who did this to me."

Michael kept his word. He got his revenge on the Pistons and Isiah Thomas in his next NBA game. Michael scored 49 points and pulled down 15 rebounds as the Bulls beat the Pistons in overtime 139–126.

The Bulls finished in third place in their division. However, any hopes of making it into the Eastern Conference finals were quickly shattered. The Milwaukee Bucks eliminated the Bulls in four games as Michael's first season came to an end.

Of the Bulls' 82 games, Michael had been the top scorer in 55! His 28.2 points per game was the team's best, and he also led the team in rebounding, assists, and steals. His season total of 2,313 points was the best in the team's history.

Remembering the previous year's college draft, Michael had the last laugh when the votes were tallied for Rookie of the Year. Of the 78 votes cast,

Michael got 57 and a half votes, 37 more than his nearest rival Hakeem Olajuwon. Sam Bowie finished a distant third.

Despite his spectacular statistics, there were still some people who weren't convinced that Michael would develop into a great player. Julius Erving himself said that truly great players could lead their teams to the top and were not one-man shows. Michael was a fine ballplayer, Dr. J said, but not yet in a league with Larry Bird or Magic Johnson.

"Bird and Magic have led their teams to championships. That's something we don't know whether Michael can do or not," Erving explained.

That criticism would become a sore point with Michael. It would dog him for the next six seasons.

8
A Tough Break

Basketball is a big man's game. It may be a sport where finesse, fancy moves, and a soft touch can win games, but it is more often than not an intensely physical game. The sport is dominated by men who stand close to seven feet tall, weigh anywhere from 220 to 285 pounds, and are as big as National Football League linebackers. Players often set picks, screens, and blocks for their teammates and the result can sometimes be bone-jarring collisions. Michael, at six-foot-six-inches and 200 pounds is far from being one of the biggest players in the NBA. However, what Michael lacks in size, he makes up for in determination and guts, especially when he heads down the lane.

A player driving down the lane, the 12-foot wide strip in front of each basket, is likely to face a barrage of body slams, flying elbows, and bruising blocks. The possibility of serious injury is ever present. The lane is no place for the timid and it takes courage and confidence to drive down it.

John Bach, the Bulls' assistant coach, once described the lane as "an alligator wrestling pond." However, it is often where the action is, and Michael never hesitated to drive down it when he thought he could score.

The 1985–86 season had brought many changes to the Bulls' lineup. There was a new coach, Stan Albeck, who had replaced Kevin Loughery. Several players had been traded away and a new rookie forward, Charles Oakley, had joined the team. Jordan made friends with Oakley right away. Tall and solidly built, the six-foot-nine-inch, 240-pound rookie was not afraid to set a screen or block for Michael and take the hit as Michael took the shot. Jordan appreciated Oakley's aggressiveness and would later jokingly refer to Oakley as his on-court "bodyguard."

If Michael had forgotten about basketball being a rough game, he got a harsh reminder from the Detroit Pistons in the second game of the season. Late in the game, the Bulls were leading by five, 103–98, when Michael saw an opening and drove hard down the lane. As Michael leapt toward the basket, Bill Laimbeer, the Pistons' six-foot-eleven-inch, 260-pound center slammed into him and knocked him to the floor. The foul was a blatant one and Michael lunged at the Detroit center. In seconds, both the Bulls' and Pistons' benches emptied in a wild demonstration of basket-brawl.

"He didn't try to block the shot," Michael later explained. "He just slammed me down. Then he just walked away. He didn't try to help me up or say he was sorry. I think he did it intentionally," Michael said angrily.

When the game resumed, Michael turned his rage into a scoring rampage. By the time the final buzzer sounded, he had scored 33 points and the Bulls were on top 121–111.

As discouraging as the hard-hitting tactics of Detroit were, Michael soon got an even worse break in the next game. Not even an on-court "bodyguard" like Charles Oakley could prevent what happened next.

Chicago was set to take on the Golden State Warriors at the Oakland Coliseum. The Warriors' lineup included Michael's Olympic teammate, Chris Mullin, and the former Georgetown scoring star, Eric "Sleepy" Floyd.

The two teams seemed evenly matched, and the first quarter was uneventful. There was less than a minute to go in the second half when Michael ran downcourt and made a sharp cut to the left. Suddenly he fell to the ground. Michael's teammates waited anxiously for Michael to get up, but he didn't. He appeared to be in great pain. As his teammates clustered around him, the team trainer examined Michael's foot. It appeared that Michael had sprained his ankle. Charles Oakley and Mike Smrek helped Michael hobble to the locker room. The Bulls went on to win the game 111–105.

The next day, the team trainer announced that the injury was a minor one and that Michael would miss three games at most. X rays failed to show any substantial injury. Still, Michael's teammates were surprised and worried when he showed up at practice on crutches the next day.

As part of his medical treatment, Michael had a CAT scan taken of his foot. The high-tech optical procedure revealed a tiny, but significant, break in a bone in his foot. The next day, the *Chicago Tribune* confirmed fans' worst fears. JORDAN WILL MISS 6 WEEKS, the headline read.

Without Michael's scoring talents, the Bulls lost eight of their next nine games. Michael was heartbroken and frustrated. "I've never gone through anything like this before," he complained. "Still, there has to be a good reason for why this is happening to me. Something good has to come out of it," he said. "I just can't think of it now."

Michael attended a few games, sitting on the sidelines in a coat and tie, cheering his teammates as they lost four games in a row. It was obvious to everyone that Michael was unhappy sitting on the sidelines. "My body could stand the crutches, but my mind couldn't stand the sidelines," he complained.

Michael's spirits picked up when a Bulls' employee bet him he couldn't sink a basket from his seat. After a few misses, Michael sank a shot. Just the feel of the ball in his hands made him feel better. Michael was also cheered by the visits of young, sometimes terminally ill, fans who had been invited to games as his guests and sat next to him on the sidelines. Michael would smile and exchange high fives with the kids and then give them a thrill by shooting at the basket from his seat before the games began. But it was obvious that he wanted to be back on court, and the sooner the better.

Michael retreated to Wilmington and Chapel Hill, where he watched Tar Heels' games with Dean Smith. He also took classes to complete the work necessary to get his degree. (While Michael never attended a formal graduation ceremony, he got his college diploma, proudly fulfilling the promise he had made to his mother two years earlier.) Michael began lifting weights and doing exercises to keep his muscles limber.

In December, Michael was examined by the Bulls' doctor, John Hefferon. The doctor thought there was a chance Michael could be playing by early January. It would depend on the results of another CAT scan to be done after Christmas. Meanwhile, Michael had to wear a cast on his foot. A Chicago newspaper proclaimed AIR JORDAN REMAINS GROUNDED.

The CAT scan confirmed Michael's worst fears and the newspaper's prediction. The bone had not healed, and the earliest Michael could play would be February. Fans wondered whether Michael would miss the entire season. Despite the fact that he had only played in three games that season, fans still voted Michael onto the All-Star team. He attended the game as a spectator.

After the cast was removed, Michael returned to North Carolina to visit his parents and friends in Chapel Hill. Unknown to the Chicago Bulls' management, Michael secretly began to play basketball at Chapel Hill. At first he began with foul shots and dribbling. Soon he was playing three-on-three games with college players. The games not only strengthened his leg and foot, but also his desire to play. In early March, Michael dunked for the first time in months. He was ecstatic.

By the second week of March, Michael was practicing with the Bulls again for the first time since October. Michael scheduled a meeting with the Bulls' owner Jerry Reinsdorf and general manager Jerry Krause to discuss his return. He also was slated to have another CAT scan performed on his foot.

The results showed that Michael's foot was not 100 percent healed. Doctors recommended that Michael call it quits for the season. If he played and reinjured the bone, there was the risk of permanent damage and his career would be jeopardized, the doctors said. No one wanted Michael to play, except Michael.

"The doctors said there was a 10 percent chance I'd reinjure it. I figured 90 percent was pretty good odds," Michael declared.

Even his own agent wanted Michael to play it safe. David Falk thought playing was an "unacceptable risk."

The Bulls' management agreed with Falk, but Michael was furious. He told reporters that the Bulls didn't want him back that season because they wanted the team to do poorly. That way, he explained, the Bulls would get a higher-round pick in the college draft that summer. The accusation made headlines in the Chicago papers.

Michael met with the Bulls' management again and demanded to play. Faced with Michael's unshakable resolve, the Bulls made a deal. Michael could return to the lineup, but only for seven minutes per half. Michael hated the terms, but had no choice but to agree.

On March 15, 15,208 fans flocked to Chicago Stadium to welcome Michael back as the Bulls took on the Milwaukee Bucks. Michael's absence had been felt. Michael had missed 64 games. Of those games, the Bulls won 21 and lost 43. Sales of Bulls' tickets had also plunged.

When Michael entered the game with six minutes left in the first half, the fans gave him a standing ovation. Michael showed he was back when he slammed in a dunk over the Bucks' seven-foot-three-inch center, Randy Breuer. Michael finished the game with 12 points. Despite Charles Oakley's 35 points and 25 rebounds, the Bulls lost 125–116.

Michael thought his performance showed he could play longer than seven minutes a half. He pleaded for ten minutes of playing time each half, but the Bulls management refused. Coach Stan Albeck was sympathetic, but he had his orders.

The Bulls surged when Michael was on the court, and faltered when he left the game. In one game against the Atlanta Hawks, the Bulls had a 96–88 point lead. After Michael left the game, the lead evaporated as the Hawks racked up 18 points to the Bulls' 2. The result was a crushing 106–98 defeat for the Bulls.

The time restrictions infuriated Michael. He complained that they were not only preventing him from giving his best, but were disrupting the team's on-court chemistry. Michael pleaded for an end to the restrictions, but the Bulls wouldn't budge.

Finally in April, the restrictions were lifted and Michael returned to the starting lineup. His presence lifted the Bulls in the season's closing weeks. He scored more than 26 points in each of the last seven games of the season, resulting in four Bulls' victories. Still, the Bulls finished with a dismal 30–52 record. Of the 16 teams to win a playoff spot, the Bulls had the poorest record.

The NBA playoffs are a step up from the regular season. The level of intensity is higher. Driven by the chance for a championship, players go all out, sometimes giving the best performances of their careers and creating some of the most memorable chapters in basketball history. Michael Jordan has written quite a few chapters in that story and has rewritten the record books more than once. However, in 1986 Michael had not yet played in a single playoff game and he was eager to make his mark.

More than 15,000 fans jammed Boston Garden for the first game of the 1986 playoffs. Celtics fans clearly expected their team to take the title. Boston fans have a reputation for being among the loudest and proudest in the league and they had plenty to be proud of, too. Celtic greats like Bob Cousy and Bill Russell made basketball history by taking their team to championships year after year in the 1950s and 1960s. The Celtics — three-time NBA champs in the 1980s — not only had Larry Bird, one of basketball's all-time greats, but solid and seasoned players like Kevin McHale, Bill Walton, and seven-foot Robert Parish.

Boston's Dennis Johnson had the job of guarding Michael. In one-on-one situations, Michael was unstoppable. The Celtics tried to double- and triple-team him, but Michael drove down the lane again and again, taking on Bird, McHale, and Parish, sometimes at the same time.

Michael made one spectacular play after another. In one, Michael went up against three Celtics defenders. He leapt into the air, making a move toward the basket from the right side. As the Celtics threw their arms up to block the shot, Michael swung the ball underneath their arms and around to the left side of the basket. He seemed to hang in midair as he spun the ball off the backboard and into the basket. Even in instant replay, the move was unbelievable.

The Bulls took a 12-point lead in Game 1, as Michael pumped in 20 of the Bulls' first 43 points. He scored 30 points in the first half, nearly matching Elgin Baylor's record of 33. In the second half, the Celtics defense smothered Michael and held him to 19 points. Boston turned on the offense and by the time the final buzzer sounded, Bird had 30 points, McHale had 27, and Robert Parish had 23. Johnson had his revenge as he scored 26 points, 24 of them in the second half. Boston won 123–104.

"Not many people like to guard Jordan," Dennis Johnson said after the game. "He's by far the best guard in the NBA."

"He's the most talented player I've seen in my eight years in the league," said Bulls' assistant coach Mike Thibault as reporters crowded the

Bulls' hot and cramped locker room. But Thibault warned that the Bulls would not be able to beat the Celtics even if Michael scored 50 points. The Bulls would need more than that. "Michael is going to have to create shots for his teammates, and they're going to have to hit them," he said.

This would not be the last time someone said that about Michael Jordan and the Bulls. In fact, Michael and the Bulls would prove the statement's accuracy in the very next game.

Michael was eager for a rematch. "Game 2 is coming up Sunday and I've got those fresh young legs," he said. "While everybody was playing, I had a 19 or 20 week vacation. I want to win badly, very badly. My season is wrapped up in these playoffs."

Once again, Dennis Johnson bore the brunt of Michael's attack, and Michael outjumped and outmaneuvered the Boston guard. Jordan demolished the rest of the Celtics' defense, dribbling between his legs, behind his back, and doing twisting turning lay-ups. He was all over the court, driving when the lane was open and hitting outside jumpers when it was not. He went one-on-one with Larry Bird and dunked over the head of Robert Parish.

"You could tell something magical was happening," said Michael's teammate, Orlando Woolridge. "He was incredible."

With just over ten seconds left in the game, Boston led 116–114. As the fans began counting down the last seconds, it appeared that the Celtics' victory was secure. Robert Parish merely had to run out the clock. But as he dribbled the ball, Michael stole it and broke downcourt. With Kevin McHale playing tight defense, Michael lofted a long last-second jump shot. It missed and the final buzzer sounded.

The Celtics fans were on their feet, cheering and proclaiming victory. The game, however, was not over. The referees had called a pushing foul on Kevin McHale. Suddenly, Boston Garden exploded with the sound of 15,000 fans booing at the tops of their lungs. Michael was awarded two foul shots. He hit both, giving him 54 points, tying the game, and sending it into overtime.

The score was again tied with just three seconds remaining in the overtime period. Michael got the ball and hurriedly launched a 15-foot jump shot, much like his legendary NCAA-championship shot. But instead of going in, the ball bounced off the rim and Bird grabbed the rebound. In the second overtime, Boston won the game 135–131.

Michael had scored 63 points, but it hadn't been enough. "We played very well," Michael said. "The game just came down to who got the breaks at the end and who didn't."

"Want to know how great Jordan is?" Boston's coach K.C. Jones asked reporters. "Normally the guys on the bench are leaning forward to make eye contact with me. When they saw what Jordan was doing, nobody wanted to guard him. I'd look down the bench and they were all leaning back."

"I wasn't guarding him," Dennis Johnson said after the game. "No one was guarding him. No one *can* guard him."

"That was the most amazing display of basketball I've ever seen," Larry Bird admitted.

The defeat in double overtime seemed to take the wind out of the Bulls' sails. In the third and final game, Kevin McHale's 31 points led the Celtics to a 122–104 victory. Boston eliminated Chicago and would go on to win the 1986 NBA championship.

Michael's three-game performance was one for the record books, though. In 1960, Wilt "The Stilt" Chamberlain had scored 116 points in three play-off games. Michael topped that mark with a 131-point performance. Michael's amazing 63-point performance in Game 2 was also a record. Elgin Baylor of the Los Angeles Lakers had scored 61 points in a playoff game against the Celtics 24 years earlier. Now Michael owned that record, but it didn't mean much to him in the face of the Bulls' defeat.

"Forget the record," he said with disappointment. "I'd give all the points back if we could win."

9
Point Man

Michael spent much of the summer of 1986 off the basketball court. For the first time in many years, he didn't work out frequently. The previous summer he had spent many hours working on his outside shot and jumpers. After his second season, he preferred to spend his time playing golf. Not only did it present less of a risk to his foot, but it also provided Michael with hours of relaxation and an escape from the increasing pressures of being an NBA star.

Michael also continued to be involved in a variety of civic and charitable activities. Basketball had brought him success and fame, and Michael was eager to find ways to give something back to those less fortunate, especially needy children.

"My childhood means a lot to me," Michael once said. Perhaps because of his own happy childhood, Michael targeted children's charities as an area where he could do some good. Prior to the start of the 1986–87 season, Michael visited several children's hospitals where his smile and charm lifted the spirits of the sick kids. In an evening visit to a children's hospital in Pittsburgh, he signed autographs for hours and set up a basketball hoop in the middle of the room. He organized a shooting contest and told the children that they couldn't go to sleep until they each made at least one basket. There were many kids who slept better that night, thanks to Michael's visit.

In another visit to a children's hospital in Tennessee, Michael was so touched by the plight of the sick children that he took out his checkbook and wrote out a $15,000 contribution right on the spot.

Despite being a celebrity, Michael remained open and friendly to his fans, especially the young ones. In fact, Michael was looking forward to receiving trick or treaters at his townhouse in the Chicago suburbs on Halloween night in 1986. He was disappointed when a preseason road trip prevented him from staying home that night. "Kids, sorry I missed you for Halloween," he wrote in a note that he taped to the door of his home. "If you still want trick or treat, come back in three days." Michael had special cards printed up that were good for free Big Mac hamburgers and he left them outside his door.

Michael was eager to start what he hoped would be a full and fruitful season. "I'm hungrier and more anxious than I was in my first year in the league," Michael told reporters.

If anyone had doubts that Michael's recovery was complete, they were quickly dispelled in the season opener. New York's Madison Square Garden was completely sold out on November 1, 1986, as the Bulls took on the Knicks. Michael's 50 points powered the Bulls to a 108–103 victory.

Michael was again the Bulls' top scorer. In one stretch in late November and early December, Michael had nine straight games in which he scored 40 or more points. In the first 62 games of the season, Michael was the team's high scorer 61 times!

In another game against the Knicks, Michael scored the Bulls' final 18 points.The Bulls were down 97–95 with just 13 seconds left. Michael dunked to tie the game 97–97. Despite being double-teamed by Gerald Wilkins and Darrell Walker, Michael dodged his defenders and raced to the basket for another score. Then with seconds left, he hit a long jump shot to win the game 101–99.

"Michael Jordan played infallible ball for the last five minutes. Eighteen points in a row during crunch time with two guys on him. What else has to be said?" asked the Knicks' coach Hubie Brown.

Although Coach Doug Collins stressed team play, he knew his offense depended on Michael's massive talents. He frequently called Michael his "nuclear weapon." However, there were some who said that Michael was a one-man show, and the Bulls a one-dimensional team.

Larry Bird was one of those players. "I don't like to watch the same guy take every shot. That's not what the game is all about," the Celtic star said. While Bird didn't mention any names, it was obvious he was talking about Michael.

Bulls' teammates like Earl Cureton acknowledged that the Bulls were the Michael Jordan show and that his teammates were merely a supporting cast. After scoring 53 point to win a game against the Portland Trail Blazers, Michael himself acknowledged this.

"I'm a little embarrassed about scoring so many points," Michael said after the game. "It's like stealing from the team, and this was a whole team effort. I just felt that because of the way things were going, any shot was going in. This is the type of game where your instincts take over."

The Bulls were set to face Charles Barkley and the Philadelphia 76ers later that month. "Sir Charles," one of the NBA's toughest and most talented players, vowed, "I won't let Michael Jordan score 40 points if I have to break him into little pieces."

Michael promptly pumped in 47 points as the Bulls won 105–89. "I was only kidding when I said that," an embarrassed Barkley said after the game when a reporter reminded him of his prediction.

As a result of his red-hot performances, Michael was the top vote-getter in the voting by the fans for the All-Star team.

One of the highlights of the All-Star Game weekend at Seattle's Kingdome Arena was the Slam-Dunk Contest. Michael delighted the crowd with a series of incredible high-flying dunks. In his most spectacular one, Michael toed the foul line, then backpedalled to the other end of the court as if plotting his takeoff. He began dribbling — tongue out — as he picked up speed. When he hit the foul line, he took off. Michael seemed to hang in mid-air as he floated toward the basket and jammed the ball through the net.

Michael finished with a slashing, sideways, tongue-wagging tomahawk dunk that gave him the victory over his nearest competitor, Jerome Kersey of Portland. What made Michael's dunks even more amazing was that nearly all of them were improvised and unplanned. "I never know what I'm going to do until I get up there," he revealed. "The adrenaline that runs through me is just unexplainable. I've just got it and hope I keep it."

Michael won the $12,500 prize money which he shared equally with his Chicago Bulls' teammates. "They worked so hard for the first half of the season," he told reporters, "and I got all the publicity."

The Slam-Dunk Contest brought Michael even greater notoriety. "That he is one of the greatest players is indisputable," Tom Brokaw said on *NBC Nightly News*. "He is also a very nice man."

Fans were going nuts for Michael. After one game in New York, fans chased the Bulls' bus, chanting Michael's name. On another occasion, a woman lay down in front of Michael's limousine. She said she didn't care if she got run over, as long as the car was Michael's.

One cold, snowy day in February, the pressure got to Michael. His twenty-fourth birthday was the next day. After a game against Sacramento, Michael called home to say he would arrive in time for dinner the next night. He hopped on a plane to North Carolina where he celebrated his birthday with family and friends. Following a quick game of golf, he hopped on a midnight plane back to Chicago. The trip home, however short, recharged his energies and brightened his mood.

Michael proceeded to go on a scoring spree for the rest of the season. In late February in a game against the New Jersey Nets, he scored 58 points and set a team record by hitting 26 of his 27 free throws. A week later in an exciting overtime victory over the Detroit Pistons, Michael scored 61 points.

On April 7, the Bulls faced the Pistons again. As usual, Detroit played a rough, physical game. Michael, as the Bulls' main ball-handler, bore the brunt of the attack. As he dribbled to the basket, Bill Laimbeer slammed Michael into the support pole for the backboard. Michael charged at Laimbeer, only to be called on a technical foul.

"I had to let him know, and let a lot of people know, that I wasn't going to take that anymore, especially when I think he did it on purpose," Michael would later say.

Michael, still seething, got his revenge by scoring 39 points to give the Bulls a 116–86 victory. Michael wondered how far things would go and what it would take to put an end to Detroit's roughhouse tactics. He had no idea that things would only get worse in the next few seasons.

In the next-to-last game of the season, Michael scored 61 points against the Atlanta Hawks. He pumped in 23 points in a row, setting an NBA record. His 61-point performance put him over the 3,000 point level for the season, making him only the second player after Wilt Chamberlain to top that mark.

Michael's season had been a resounding comeback. He was the NBA's top scorer, averaging 37.1 points per game for a season total of 3,041. He had a good season defensively, blocking 100 shots and finishing second in steals. "I'm very happy with my season," Michael said. "I'm surprised I scored this many points. I don't think I'll ever have a season like this offensively. You know, maybe this will be the greatest season I ever have."

While Michael was a one-man scoring sensation, some writers said that the Bulls lacked the depth necessary to put together a versatile, well-rounded offense. They claimed Michael's one-on-one style, as spectacular as it was, didn't allow his teammates to contribute and develop into scorers. What angered Michael most were the people who said that Michael's pursuit of scoring titles prevented a full-fledged team effort. Michael bristled when opposing players and sportswriters called the Bulls "Team Jordan," and "The Jordanaires."

You might think that any team with the league's leading scorer would have a better chance at winning the NBA championship. In fact, the opposite is true. Few teams had ever won an NBA championship with the league's leading scorer in their lineup. Kareem Adbul-Jabbar and the Milwaukee Bucks had done it in 1971, but no team had done it since. The teams that won the most championships nearly always had at least two players who could consistently score 20 or more points per game. Michael knew this and he pressed the Bulls'

91

management to obtain other ball players who could score consistently.

The team drafted Horace Grant, a six-foot-ten-inch, 210-pound forward from Clemson University. Grant, who had grown up in a small town in Georgia, had led his conference in scoring and rebounding. (His twin brother Harvey plays for the Washington Bullets.) The Bulls had also traded a draft pick to obtain Scottie Pippen, a six-foot-seven-inch forward who had averaged 26.3 points while playing in his final year at a small college, Central Arkansas University. Pippen, one of twelve children who had grown up in poverty in Hamburg, Arkansas, had the desire and the talent, but no one knew for sure what it would take to turn the Bulls into winners.

More than 18,680 fans packed Chicago Stadium for the 1987–88 season opener against the Philadelphia 76ers. Michael pumped in 36 points to sink the Sixers 104–94. Scottie Pippen proved to be a good ball-handler and shooter, and the Bulls stampeded to a 9–2 record by Thanksgiving. Michael seemed to be playing differently, utilizing his defensive skills more. He did score 34 in a 98–86 Bulls' win over the Houston Rockets, but he also blocked five shots, including two by Houston's "Twin Towers," the seven-foot Hakeem Olajuwon and the seven-foot-four-inch Ralph Sampson.

"I wanted to show that I can play defense and that I don't shoot as much as Larry Bird would say," Michael stated.

The Bulls came into Salt Lake City, Utah, on December 2 to take on the Jazz. In the middle of the game, Michael drove downcourt on John Stockton, the Jazz's six-foot-two-inch guard. Michael slammed a towering dunk right over his head. Larry Miller, the owner of the Jazz, was sitting at courtside.

"Why don't you pick on someone your own size?" Miller screamed.

On the next play, Michael drove downcourt again. This time seven-foot, 290-pound Mel Turpin blocked his path. Michael went up against Turpin and slammed a dunk over the Jazz center.

"Was he big enough?" Michael taunted Miller as he ran past the Jazz owner.

Detroit had beaten the Bulls in an exciting game in December and were ready to do it again when they met in January. In the third period, the Bulls were ahead 57–52. As Michael jumped to grab a rebound, Rick Mahorn, the Pistons' six-foot-ten-inch, 255-pound forward, grabbed Michael and threw him to the ground. Suddenly, both benches emptied in a free-for-all. When things settled down, the Bulls went on a tear. Michael ended up with 36 points, 10 rebounds, and 10 assists — a triple double (double figures in three categories). The Bulls whipped the Pistons 115–99, but Michael was upset.

"I understand he had to stop me, but not to the point he had to throw me to the floor, not knowing if I'd get hurt or not," Michael said in the locker room later.

"If you drive into the lane," a Detroit player responded, "you're going to get fouled."

The All-Star Game provided a well-needed break

for Michael and the Bulls. The All-Star festivities were set to take place at Chicago Stadium, and Chicago fans were expecting a great show. Michael gave them one.

He won his second Slam-Dunk Competition with a "Kiss the Rim" slam dunk. Michael said the high-flying face-to-the-rim jam was a tribute to his idol, Dr. J. In the All-Star Game itself, Michael scored 40 and won the game's Most Valuable Player award.

Easter came early in 1988, on April 3. In Detroit, the winter winds had been replaced by warm spring breezes as eager fans streamed into the Pistons' home arena, the Palace at Auburn Hills. The game was one of the most hotly anticipated games of the season. Many fans expected the game to be a preview of the playoffs.

Michael as usual went all out. When Detroit's defenders blocked the lane, Michael hit long outside jumpers. If Michael had had a weak outside shot early in his career, years of constant practice had changed that dramatically. The Pistons tried tight man-to-man defense, pitting Isiah Thomas or defensive ace Joe Dumars against Michael. It didn't matter. Michael was unstoppable. He missed just 4 of his first 24 shots. By the time the first half ended, Michael had 32 points. "He was on fire," said Detroit's Vinnie Johnson.

The Pistons tried to double-team Michael in the second half. Dennis Rodman, Detroit's hard-charging rebounding specialist, would often leave his man to triple-team Michael. It didn't work. Michael still scored 27 in the second half.

The score stood 110–110 as Isiah Thomas got the ball with just 24 seconds left. Thomas tried to get a shot off, but Michael blocked it. With just four seconds remaining, Michael was fouled and awarded two shots. He made them both, and the Bulls won 112–110. Michael had scored 59 points.

After the game, the Pistons' players and coaching staff were furious. They had to do something to shut Jordan down if they were to beat the Bulls in the playoffs.

"We made up our minds right then and there that Michael Jordan was not going to beat us by himself again," said Detroit's coach Chuck Daly.

The Pistons began working on defensive strategies to ground Air Jordan. Plans and plays were drawn up with the secrecy of a military campaign.

The Bulls finished the season with a 50–32 record, good for second place. It was the team's best record in thirteen years and it qualified the Bulls for a spot in the playoffs.

The Bulls' foe in the first round of the playoffs was the Cleveland Cavaliers. They were a formidable team who had beaten the Bulls three times that season.

Craig Ehlo, the Cavs' six-foot-seven-inch forward, drew the unfortunate assignment of having to guard Michael. He seemed to be powerless to stop the raging Bull as Michael scored 50 points and the Bulls won the opener 104–93.

After drawing the assignment to guard against Michael in the next game, Cleveland guard Ron Harper taunted Ehlo, boasting, "Michael Jordan will never score 50 against me." He was only half-right. Michael scored 55 as the Bulls won 106–101. Michael's back-to-back 50-plus point playoff games was an NBA first.

The series returned to the Cavs' home ground, the Richfield Coliseum. Pumped up by the Cleveland crowd, the Cavs bounced back in the next two games, winning twice despite Michael's 38-point and 44-point performances. Michael had played with a sore back and aching knee, but refused to be sidelined.

The Cavs roared to an 18-point lead in the first period of Game 5. Michael was plagued by turnovers, losing the ball seven times. But the Bulls fought back. With the Cavs ahead 41–37, Scottie Pippen saw Michael cut toward the basket. He lofted a pass toward the hoop. Michael jumped and caught the ball as it neared the rim. Then he slammed it through the hoop on the way down for a perfect alley-oop play. Pippen would eventually score 24 as the Bulls won the game 107–101, and the first round of the playoffs. While Michael's 45.2 average for the five game series was an NBA record, Pippen's performance proved he could be a potent offensive weapon in Chicago's attack. While it didn't exactly kill off the "one-man team" criticism, it briefly took the spotlight off Michael.

"Now we know we're not a one-man team or Team Jordan anymore," Pippen proudly told reporters.

Detroit, as expected, was the Bulls' next foe.

"We're going to make Michael work for everything," Joe Dumars promised, and he was right. The Pistons' aggressive defense had earned them the nickname of basketball's "Bad Boys," and they were prepared to live up to the name. They used their big men — Bill Laimbeer and Rick Mahorn — to clog the lane and force Michael to the outside. Isiah Thomas, Joe Dumars, and Dennis Rodman also teamed up to harass Michael and keep him out of shooting range.

Detroit kept up a withering and wearying defensive attack on Michael. The Bulls' star seemed tired. And his shooting game suffered, too. In Game 1, he missed 10 of 16 shots as Detroit won 93–82. In Game 3, he was so unnerved he didn't score his first point until 18 minutes into the game. Detroit was wreaking its revenge for the Easter massacre Michael had inflicted on them earlier in the season. The Pistons routed the Bulls 101–79 and went on to eliminate Chicago, 4 games to 1.

Despite the fact that Chicago had made it past the first round of the playoffs for the first time since 1981, the defeats stung the team's pride. The humiliation was only increased the next day when the *Detroit Free Press* revealed the Pistons' defensive strategy. The newspaper featured charts and plays that showed how Detroit had grounded Air Jordan. The plans were eagerly studied by countless NBA coaches that summer and, by the next season, the plan had a name — The Jordan Rules.

Despite the drubbing the Bulls took from Detroit, it had been a remarkable season for Michael. He was once again the NBA's leading scorer with a 35-point-per-game average. He was first in steals, too, with 259. Michael was the only player in NBA history to lead the league in both scoring and steals. Michael was especially proud to be named the NBA Defensive Player of the Year.

Michael was also named the NBA Most Valuable Player. He won 47 first-place votes while his nearest rival, Larry Bird, got 16. "I can think of no better way to cap the season," Michael said. "It was one of the goals I set for myself at the beginning of the season."

Michael signed a new eight-year contract with the Bulls that would pay him $25 million. While few NBA superstars commanded such a high salary, few players were as skilled, consistent, and popular as Michael. Michael's contribution to the Bulls' success was indisputable. From 1987 to 1989, the Bulls sold out more games than they had in the previous 22 years. From 1983 to 1988, NBA revenues had doubled and Michael deserved some of the credit for that, too. In cities where NBA teams had experienced poor attendance, games would now sell out when the Bulls came to town. Indiana Pacers' executive Donnie Walsh spoke for all the teams when he said, "We should all be chipping in to pay him. He does so much for the league."

10
Charging Bulls

"**M**ichael plays it down, but he's a one-man team."

The speaker was Michael's former Tar Heels' teammate, Sam Perkins of the Dallas Mavericks. As the 1988–89 season began, Michael heard that comment more and more. No one disputed that Michael had incredible athletic abilities. But around the NBA, players and writers said that Michael hadn't improved his teammates level of play like Larry Bird or Magic Johnson had. They were team players who had brought their teams championships. Michael, they said, hadn't done that. Michael pointed out that Magic was surrounded with talented players like Kareem Abdul-Jabbar and James Worthy. Bird had Kevin McHale and many other supporting stars. Michael asked if either the Lakers or the Celtics would have won with Bird and Magic alone. He was right, but his answers failed to quiet the critics.

Fans had a higher opinion of Michael. When the

Bulls came to New York City on Election Day 1988, fans unfurled a huge sign from the balcony in Madison Square Garden that read, MICHAEL FOR PRESIDENT. The cheers were louder for Michael than for any of the home-team players.

Michael continued to put together big numbers, but not always with successful results. He scored 52 points against Denver, but the Bulls lost anyway. Slowly, the Bulls were beginning to get more points from other players like John Paxson, an All-American out of Notre Dame, guard Sam Vincent, and Brad Sellers, but rarely in the same game. Still, when the team's offense sputtered, the Bulls would often lose, no matter how many Michael scored. Michael had his season high with 53 on January 21, 1989, against the Phoenix Suns, but the Bulls were defeated 116–107.

Michael scored his 10,000th career point at the Spectrum in Philadelphia on January 25. Only Wilt Chamberlain had reached the 10,000-point mark faster. Michael ended the game with 33 points, but the Bulls lost 120–108. Michael hated losing, and it was small consolation that he was named the top vote-getter in the balloting for the All-Star team with more than one million votes.

The fact that Michael was carrying the team worried the Bulls' management. He was averaging more than 40 minutes of playing time per game. He had tremendous stamina, but Coach Doug Collins and others in the Bulls' management were concerned that Michael was tiring himself out. Michael was aware of this, but it didn't cause him any concern.

"I never try to pace myself," Michael said. "I know a lot of people think I'll wear myself down. Someday I may burn out physically, but the desire will always burn. I'll go at full speed until I give out."

All of the Chicago Bulls underwent regular medical examinations to monitor their physical conditions. Many top athletes have 7 to 10 percent of their body weight as fat. Tests showed Michael had just 3 percent. Michael was in great shape despite a diet that in the early part of his career was filled with fast-food favorites like hamburgers and fried chicken. Currently, Michael prefers to "pig out on pasta."

Other players in the league wondered how long Michael could keep up his intense pace.

"Michael plays every game like it's his last," noted Glenn "Doc" Rivers, then with the Atlanta Hawks. Dominique Wilkins, also of the Hawks, suggested that Michael might be in danger of shortening his career.

Coach Doug Collins wanted to limit Michael to 37 minutes per game. Before he could do that, however, the other Bulls had to score, and score consistently. Collins tried shifting Michael from his position as shooting guard to point guard. The role of the point guard is to bring the ball down-court and be a playmaker. Collins hoped that Michael would use his ball-handling skills to find and hit the open man with passes and help create a balanced scoring attack. At times it worked. Bill Cartwright scored 20 points to lead the Bulls to a win against Seattle in March. Scottie Pippen led the Bulls in scoring twice that month, too. All three games resulted in Bulls' victories.

Other times, the strategy failed and Michael took it upon himself to shoot and score more. In the first week of April, Michael scored 31, 40, 40, 47, 29, and 22 points in six games. The rest of the Bulls were ice-cold and the Bulls lost all six games. Michael ended the season as NBA scoring champ for the third consecutive time with a 32.5 average. The Bulls finished in fifth place with a 47–35 record.

Chicago qualified for the playoffs and faced the Cleveland Cavaliers in the first round, a best-of-five series. The Cavs had beaten the Bulls six times that season.

The Bulls broke their losing streak in the first game, but the Cavs quickly evened the series. After two more games, the series was tied 2-2. The deciding game was scheduled for Cleveland's home court, the Richfield Coliseum.

Michael was booed loudly as introductions were made before the game. Michael took the booing as just another challenge. Michael responded with a second-half scoring burst that gave Chicago a late-game lead. However, Craig Ehlo scored to put Cleveland ahead 100–99 with just three seconds left.

The Bulls called time-out. It was time for "The Archangel Offense." "That's where we give the ball to Michael and say, 'Save us,'" Bulls' assistant coach John Bach explained.

When play resumed, Brad Sellers passed the ball in at half-court to Michael. Michael dribbled twice, and found an opening at the top of the key. Craig Ehlo and Larry Nance lunged at him, but Michael got off a 16-foot jump shot. Suddenly, as the ball flew toward the basket, complete silence fell over the Cleveland crowd. The game's final buzzer sounded as the ball sailed through the net. Michael leapt high into the air as he repeatedly pumped his fist in the air. The Bulls had won 101–100.

"I never saw it go in, but I knew right away from the crowd reaction — silence — that it was good," Michael said with relief in the locker room. History had repeated itself once again. Michael had saved the day with a last-second jump shot.

The Knicks were next. Michael pulled a groin muscle in the third game of the best-of-seven series and played in pain for most of the match. He still scored 40 points as the Bulls won the game 111–88 to take a 2–1 lead in the series.

Fans and reporters began gathering outside Chicago Stadium around 10 o'clock on Sunday morning in anticipation of Game 4. It was a warm spring day and there was excitement in the air.

"There he is!" a fan yelled out as a sleek red Ferrari slammed to a stop in the players' parking area. No one had to guess the identity of the car's owner. There, on the North Carolina license plate, under the motto First in Flight, was the telltale M-AIR-J.

The door opened, and out stepped Michael Jordan wearing black pants, a white sweater, and black loafers with no socks. Michael gave the fans a smile and bantered with the reporters. When asked if the groin injury would prevent him from playing, Michael shook his head.

"I'll play sore," he replied, "but I'll play."

"You tired?" a reporter asked.

Michael grinned. "Never tired when you're about to win a series."

When Michael walked onto the court, he walked with a noticeable limp. He moved slowly in the opening minutes of the game. He lacked his usual speed and seemed unable to jump as high as he usually did. Still, he produced eight points in the first period.

Having tested the injury in the first quarter, Michael relaxed in the second and played with more confidence. Within minutes, it was "full speed ahead," as Michael would later say. The Knicks tried to contain Michael with a full-court press. Michael cut through his defenders, breaking into the open in a style that reminded observers of the great Chicago Bears' running back Gale Sayers. Feeling stronger, Michael took to the air for a series of head-spinning, gravity-defying dunks, and reverse lay-ups.

The Bulls went on a 25-point tear in the last period. Michael accounted for 18 of those points. He ended up with 47 points, as the Bulls won 106–93.

Michael had forgotten about his injury. "It's the playoffs," he exclaimed in the locker room. "It's not time to be injured. It's not time to think about it."

After the Knicks won the next game, the series stood at 3 games to 2 in favor of Chicago. In Game

6, the Knicks looked as if they would snatch a victory from the jaws of defeat. The Bulls were ahead 111–107 with under two minutes to go. Patrick Ewing fired a pass to Trent Tucker who launched a 27-foot jump shot. As he let go of the ball, Chicago's Craig Hodges slammed into him. The referee blew his whistle as Tucker's shot fell through the net. It was good, and a three-point shot as well. Tucker went to the foul line and turned it into a rare four-point play. The game was tied 111–111.

The Bulls were ready to go with the Archangel Offense again. Michael got the ball with just four seconds to go when he was fouled. Michael sank both foul shots, giving Chicago the victory and the series. It had clearly been a team effort with Scottie Pippen contributing 19 points, Cartwright 16, Craig Hodges 15, and Horace Grant 11. But the series belonged to Michael. He had scored 214 points in the six-game series, averaging 35.6 points.

"Michael Jordan is the best player to ever put on a uniform," then New York Knicks' coach Rick Pitino declared.

The Bulls' next foe, the Pistons, were definitely not as impressed with Michael. Detroit had defeated the Bulls six times during the season and the Pistons were hungry for the NBA title, too. The previous season, they'd almost won it, but were beaten by the Lakers in a fierce seven-game series. The Pistons felt their time had come and they expected to make short work of the Bulls. Detroit's strategy for winning was simple: Stop Jordan.

The plan failed in Game 1. Detroit had a one-point lead late in the game when Michael suddenly found his range and began hitting shot after shot. By the final buzzer, Michael had 32 points and the Pistons were in shock. They had lost 94–88.

A case of the flu slowed Michael down in the next game, and Detroit won to even the series. Michael shook off the flu and scored 46 points in the third game, despite Joe Dumar's tough defense. The score was tied 97–97 with just 3 seconds left. Michael broke away from Detroit's defenders and popped in a last-second shot to win the game 99–97. Michael bragged after the game that he had stolen the victory right out of the Pistons' hands.

In the next game, the Pistons made Michael pay for his cockiness. Detroit harassed and double-teamed Michael and used their big men to push him out of scoring range. The Jordan Rules worked with a vengeance as Michael missed seven of nine shots in the first period. The rest of the Bulls seemed intimidated by the Pistons' hard-hitting defense, and Detroit won the game 86–80. In the following game, the Pistons held Michael to 13 points and won again. Chicago faded in the face of Detroit's aggressive attack. Despite Michael's 32 points in Game 6, the Pistons emerged with a 103–94 victory and eliminated the Bulls. Detroit went on to sweep the Lakers in four games for the NBA crown.

Try as he might, Michael could not overcome The Jordan Rules, at least not yet.

11
Fame and Fortune

For years, Michael had been considered Chicago's most eligible bachelor. He had dated Kim Gallagher, a silver-medal winner in the 1984 Olympics and his name had been linked in the press to that of actress Robin Givens. Beautiful models and actresses would often invite him to dinner or out for a date. Despite his fame, Michael was still somewhat shy. He was more interested in sports than socializing.

"Basketball," he had often said, "is my wife."

"People may think this sounds crazy but it was sometimes hard for me to meet the right girls," Michael said. "You're always wondering if they want to be with you because you're a pro ball player making a lot of money. How can you be sure they really like you for who you are?"

Michael did have a special girlfriend whom he dated for several years. Several years earlier at a Bennigan's restaurant on Michigan Avenue in Chicago, Michael was introduced to an attractive young woman named Juanita Vanoy. Juanita worked as a secretary and was not a very big basketball fan. She was less impressed with Michael's stardom than with his friendly smile and easygoing manner.

"That's what I liked about her, that she really cared for me as a person, not because I played for the Bulls," he would say later.

Michael really enjoyed being around Juanita and the pair had dated since his second season. They had been engaged for several years and decided to get married. They did so in a 3:00 A.M. secret ceremony in Las Vegas in the summer of 1989. The night owls still out on the Las Vegas streets saw Michael and Juanita, both dressed in blue jeans, step out of a limousine in front of The Little White Wedding Chapel. Surrounded by a small group of close friends, Michael and Juanita exchanged vows and rings. Later that day, the pair flew to San Diego where Michael made an appearance at a charity golf tournament to benefit the United Negro College Fund.

Michael looked forward to not only building a home life with Juanita, but also a family. Michael had always been accessible to the press and public and he received countless invitations for all kinds of charity events. When he returned to Chicago to begin the 1989–90 season, Michael called a press conference. He announced that he would be cutting back on his interviews and public appearances. He also announced that he was forming The Michael Jordan Foundation.

Deloris Jordan had been telling her son that with

his influence, image, and money, he could be a powerful force to raise money for worthy causes. Michael hoped his foundation could also be a bridge between his favorite charities and the companies with whom he worked. A key goal would be to support educational organizations, like the United Negro College Fund. Another aim would be to help sick and physically challenged children. One of the foundation's first alliances was with the Make a Wish Foundation, a group that tries to grant the last wishes of children who have incurable diseases. Michael had always had a soft spot for these children and he hoped his foundation could help them in a variety of ways. Michael announced that his mother would be the head of the operation.

While Michael kept a low profile and didn't seek credit or praise for his charity work, he and Deloris had constant discussions about the foundation's goals and activities. "Michael is all about giving back," Deloris said.

Back in the world of basketball, the Bulls once again had a new head coach, Phil Jackson. Jackson, a member of the New York Knicks championship team of 1973, was a firm believer in team play. But, like his predecessors, he also was convinced that Michael was his most potent weapon. Michael confirmed that in the first game of the season, a 124–119 overtime win against Cleveland. Michael poured in 54 points and gave the rookie coach his first NBA win.

Under Jackson, the Bulls also continued to develop as a team. Scottie Pippen was turning into a dependable scorer. John Paxson, who at six-foot-two-inches, was among the shorter players in the league, was an excellent defensive player and a strong shooter when he got the chance. The Bulls bench, too, was gaining depth. B.J. Armstrong, a baby-faced six-foot-two-inch rookie guard out of the University of Iowa, surprised everyone with a team-high 20-point performance against Philadelphia in December. From November 7 to January 23, the Bulls won 15 home games in a row, setting a new team record. By the All-Star break, the Bulls had charged to second place in their division behind the Detroit Pistons.

Through his foundation, Michael often had special guests — sick or physically challenged children — attend Bulls games and sit near the team on the sidelines. When the Bulls met the Charlotte Hornets in January, Michael set up a special basketball clinic for local children. At his own expense, Michael bought and gave away fifty tickets to the youngsters for that night's game. He put on a show, too, scoring 45 points as the Bulls stung the Hornets 107–95.

Despite Michael's intention to be less accessible to the public, Michael could never let down a fan, especially a young one. Following a game in February, a young fan and his father stood outside the Bulls' locker room in Chicago Stadium. The boy was wearing a Michael Jordan T-shirt, a Bulls' hat, and he clutched a Michael Jordan poster in his hand. Michael stepped out of the locker room and headed down the hall.

"Mr. Jordan," the boy's father said. "Can I take a picture of you with my son?"

"Sure," Michael responded. Michael stood next to the boy, and draped his arm on the boy's shoulder. The father fumbled with his camera, but it wouldn't work. The man tried to wind the film, but it didn't help. The camera was jammed. Some superstars might have walked away at that point, but Michael waited patiently, chatting amiably with the nervous, but obviously thrilled, boy. Finally after five minutes, the man got the camera working again. Michael gave a big smile as the camera's flash exploded.

"See ya," Michael said as he walked down the hall.

As usual, Michael Jordan was named to the All-Star team. But for the first time in his career, he had a teammate to keep him company. Scottie Pippen was also named to the All-Star squad.

The Bulls clinched a spot in the playoffs in late March following an exciting 118–113 overtime victory over the Cleveland Cavaliers. Michael had the best game of his career, scoring 69 points. He was deadly from the floor, making 23 of his 37 shots. From the foul line, he was even better, missing just two of his 23 free throws. Michael was a ball of energy, talking to himself on the court, saying, "Don't stop, don't stop," as he sank shot after shot.

After the game Craig Ehlo, who had the daunting task of guarding Michael, joked, "I held him under 70."

"It was one of those nights where everything

went right. I got on a roll early and found myself in great rhythm. It was definitely fun," Michael bubbled.

"This would have to be my greatest game," he added. "When I scored 63 against Boston, we lost. It sure feels a lot better."

The Bulls finished the season in second place with a 55–27 record, the team's best finish since 1972. The Bulls qualified for the playoffs and quickly breezed past the Milwaukee Bucks in the first round and faced the Philadelphia 76ers in the Eastern Conference semifinals.

Michael turned into a postseason cyclone. His 39 points sank the Sixers in the first game. His 45 points brought the Bulls back from a near-defeat to win Game 2, 101–96. Michael scored 49 in Game 3, but the 76ers, buoyed by the Philadelphia fans, won the match 118–112.

Game 4 took place on Sunday, May 13, Mother's Day. Deloris Jordan, wearing the corsage Michael had given her, sat in the stands watching as Michael scored 18 in the final quarter to power the Bulls to a come-from-behind victory 111–101. The press dubbed the game "The Mother's Day Massacre." Three days later, the Bulls coasted to a 117–99 victory in the final game and eliminated the Sixers.

Detroit, the defending NBA champions, viewed Chicago as a nuisance on their way to a second championship. They had eliminated Chicago from the playoffs two years running. With The Jordan Rules in effect, they were confident they could shut down Michael and the Bulls again. They did exactly that in the first game, beating the Bulls 86–77.

Chicago stumbled in the second game, falling behind 53–38 at the half. In the locker room, Michael lost his temper. He kicked a few chairs and the water cooler. If his teammates expected to win, Michael shouted, they'd better start playing like champions.

Michael's frustration only grew in the second half. His back ached from the constant hits he was taking from Dennis Rodman and John Salley. The final score, Detroit 102–Chicago 93, hurt even more.

The Bulls had the home-court advantage in Game 3. Galvanized by the cheering Chicago fans, Michael scored 47 points and Scottie Pippen contributed 29 points to lead the Bulls to a 107–102 victory. Pippen credited Michael's halftime tirade in the previous game as the factor that had sparked the Bulls' rally. Pippen called the speech, "Michael's wake-up call."

"Today we showed the Pistons Jordan Rules, instead of Rules Against Jordan," Phil Jackson said happily.

The series was tied at 3–3, and the final deciding game was scheduled for Detroit's home court. During the pregame shooting drills, Scottie Pippen began blinking furiously and rubbing his eyes. His vision was blurred and a stabbing pain seared through his head. Pippen was plagued by a painful migraine headache that would only get worse as the game got underway.

The Pistons' defense focused on Michael with

seven-foot-one-inch, 250-pound James Edwards and six-foot-eight-inch Dennis Rodman constantly forcing him outside. Michael's shooting was all that was keeping the Bulls in the game. Horace Grant missed fourteen of his seventeen shots. Pippen was even worse, hitting just one of ten before the pain from his headache forced him out of the game.

Detroit's depth made all the difference. Isiah Thomas had 21 points, Mark Aguirre 15, Dennis Rodman 13, and John Salley 14. Detroit won the game 93–74 and the Eastern Conference title.

"They may have the best player," Bill Laimbeer said of Michael Jordan. "We have the better team," he gloated. Laimbeer was right. Detroit won the NBA title again, whipping the Portland Trail Blazers four games to one.

Michael learned once again that one player couldn't do it all. He was convinced that if his teammates didn't start coming alive on offense, the Bulls were doomed to be also-rans year after year. Next year, Michael vowed, would be different.

12
An Air of Greatness

Michael Jordan is one of the most analyzed basketball players in the history of the game. Opposing coaches study his moves in game films, commentators analyze them on TV, and scientists have even written studies focusing on Michael's amazing abilities. No subject has aroused more interest than Michael's "hang time."

When Michael Jordan jumps, an observer can see his powerful and well-defined thigh and calf muscles bulging and straining. His legs are like those of a world-class high jumper. One expert estimated that when Michael leaps, his legs propel him off the floor with 500 to 600 pounds of pressure. His leap has been measured, and it's been shown that Michael is capable of leaping 44 inches off the ground. Combined with Michael's speed and almost acrobatic ability to twist and turn while airborne, it appears that Michael can really fly. No wonder some people dubbed Michael, "Superman in Shorts."

An Air Force professor of physics, Lieutenant Colonel Douglas Kirkpatrick, studied Michael's hang time. He calculated the time in each game Michael was in the air. He determined that in Michael's first five seasons, the Chicago Bulls star was aloft more than 90 minutes!

Michael is like a "human helicopter," another observer wrote. "His upper body seems to float near the basket, while his defenders gradually fall away."

"The only thing that stays in the air longer," joked Magic Johnson, "is an airplane."

Michael himself says, "I don't know about hang time. I think it's more or less a motion that makes it look like you're hanging. That's something I tend to have more of than other people. The motion of my legs and my arms, and my acrobatics look as though I'm hanging in the air longer than normal. But I don't think I am."

Once in the air, Michael's quick hands and flexibility allow him to improvise amazing shots as opportunities arise. "I just make them up," he says. "I usually go up for a normal shot, but after that, I don't have any plans. I never practice those moves. I don't know how I do them. It's amazing."

Michael has one of the fastest pairs of hands in basketball. That not only helps him steal the ball while playing defense, but also to control it on offense when he's dribbling or shooting. Michael's large hands and powerful grip allow him to maneuver the ball in midair and carry it over the rim or spin it off the backboard with pinpoint precision. "Michael has great hands," says NBA coach

Bill Fitch. "If Nike made gloves, they'd make a lot of money."

Michael also has an uncanny ability to cut through a crowded court of defenders when there appears to be no room. "Michael can get through cracks in the defense that other players can't even see," says John Bach, the Bulls' assistant coach. "He can knife through there when there isn't room for a firefly."

As the 1990–91 season approached, Michael pushed the Bulls hard in preseason practices and exhibition games. He played with a single-minded intensity in scrimmages and drills, trying to pump the Bulls up. He blocked his teammates' shots and stole the ball when they got careless. If the Bulls were ever going to win the championship, Michael said, they would have to play as hard as he did.

The Chicago press was convinced this would be the year the Bulls went all the way. Coach Phil Jackson saw the prediction as bad news. The last thing the Bulls needed, he warned, was to become convinced they were champions before the season had even begun. He knew the season would be a tough one for not only the Bulls, but for himself.

Jackson's toughest challenge was having to blend the talents of the team with Michael's individual skills. He knew it would not be an easy task.

Jackson wasn't encouraged by what he saw as the season began. It appeared as if the Bulls would have another frustrating year; Chicago lost their first three games. The Bulls finally won their first game, a match against the mediocre Minnesota

Timberwolves. Michael and Horace Grant led the Bulls in scoring with a less-than-impressive 17 points each. Grant had spent the previous summer doing extensive weight training. He had put on 20 pounds of muscle, and the 235-pound forward had become an excellent shot blocker and one of the Bulls' best rebounders. Michael, too, had stepped up his weight-training program to build up strength for his battles with the league's big men.

The Bulls won three games in a row on the road and seemed to be playing more as a team. In November, John Paxson led the Bulls to a 105–97 win over the Clippers. Michael Jordan was double-teamed the whole game and was held to just 14 points. It was his lowest point total in three years. Paxson was free as a result of the double-team, and the sure-shooting guard rose to the occasion with 26 points.

The Bulls had honed their defensive skills and had developed into a quick, sure-handed team. They were stealing the ball from opponents and blocking shots as never before. The defensive onslaught was rattling opponents, and the Bulls frequently held opponents to less than 100 points per game.

In early December as the frigid winter winds swirled around Chicago Stadium, the Bulls routed the Phoenix Suns 155–127. It was the highest number of points the Bulls had ever scored in the team's history. A week later, the Bulls humiliated the Cavaliers by holding Cleveland to just 5 points in the first quarter as Chicago roared to a 36–5 lead and a 116–98 victory. The Bulls continued to gain momentum winning 10 of 11 games at home in December.

Michael received a special Christmas present in the early morning hours of December 25. Juanita gave birth to their second son, Marcus James Jordan. Jeffrey Michael Jordan, Michael and Juanita's older son, had been born on November 18, 1988, and Michael loved the feeling of being a family man. "I'm so proud of being a father. The feeling is indescribable," Michael exclaimed.

The Bulls celebrated the new year by moving into first place in the Central Division. Michael reached a personal milestone at the Philadelphia Spectrum in a nationally televised game on January 9. There were 30 seconds left in the first quarter when Michael was fouled. He moved to the free-throw line. Michael knew what the shot meant. He had 14,999 career points. One more would put him in a special class. Michael made the shot, reaching the 15,000 mark in his four hundred sixtieth game. The only player to reach the 15,000 point mark faster was Wilt Chamberlain who did it in 358 games. The 18,000 fans screamed, stomped, whistled, and gave Michael a standing ovation. The air in the Spectrum was hot that night, but Michael felt chills running down his back.

"To do that on the road, and see people respect you that much, it really inspires me," Michael said.

Michael was averaging around 30 points per game. To Coach Phil Jackson, however, Michael's scoring ability was both a blessing and a curse. Jackson knew the Bulls' success had largely been a result of Michael's scoring talents. He also considered Michael to be the best player in the game. But he firmly believed that a group effort was necessary to win a championship.

Michael not only had the power to inspire his teammates. He could infuriate them, too. Some of the Bulls resented Michael's role. It was not just because Michael dominated the offense. They also felt that Michael received special treatment from the Bulls' coaching staff.

Jackson didn't deny it. Sometimes Michael's celebrity status — and the fact that he was mobbed everywhere he went — forced the Bulls' coaches to bend some of the team rules for Michael.

"There is a difference in the way he is treated," Jackson admitted. "But there is also a difference in the way he produces. A big difference."

Jackson wanted Michael to conform to the triple-post offensive system devised by assistant coach Tex Winter. In it, the Bulls were to form triangles on either side of the court and pass the ball around to find the open man. It was supposed to produce a more balanced team approach to shooting and scoring. Michael tried to play within the system, but felt it held him back sometimes.

Michael had begun to feel that time was running out for the Bulls' chance at a championship. "If we start losing, I am going to start shooting," he promised.

Michael did just that when it appeared that the rest of the Bulls were not able to produce the points needed to win.

As a result, there were times during the 1990–

91 season when some of the Bulls grew frustrated by Michael's domination of their offense. More than once, a few of Michael's teammates would say the Bulls were not playing basketball. They were playing "Michaelball."

Jackson struggled to make the triple-post system work and make the most of Michael's talents at the same time. Michael began to accept the system and his role within it as the season progressed. He began passing more and using his excellent ball-handling skills to get the ball to his teammates more often. Michael himself noticed a difference from previous seasons.

"My role has changed this season," he said. "I've accepted being leader of this team. That meant making sacrifices, not taking as many shots. But as long as we're winning, that's all that counts."

When the fans' votes for the All-Star team were counted in January, Michael was the top vote-getter for the fifth straight season. He was again the only player to win more than one million votes.

The Bulls had an 11-game winning streak when they came into Indianapolis on March 2 for a game againt the Indiana Pacers. The Pacers put pressure on Michael and held him to just 22 points. Reggie Miller, the Pacers' guard, scored 40, as the Bulls lost 135–114. The loss hurt, but Reggie Miller's words hurt even more.

"Take Michael Jordan off the team and who do they have? Nobody. Michael Jordan makes the team."

The Bulls got their revenge three weeks later as they whipped the Pacers 133–119. Michael scored

39 and John Paxson chipped in 25 points. Paxson's game was quite a performance for a "nobody."

Off the court, Michael and his mother were busier than ever with The Michael Jordan Foundation. The foundation and the Jordans found a way to help students in the Bulls' backyard.

In the spring of 1991, The Michael Jordan Foundation "adopted" a Chicago elementary school, the Edward T. Hartigan School. The school is an ordinary looking brick building in a poor Chicago neighborhood. Most of the students at the school come from the Robert Taylor Homes, an inner-city housing project. Despite its bleak surroundings, Michael and the foundation saw a special spark and spirit at the school.

"Our students do not fit the image of typical inner-city kids," says Betty Greer, the school's principal. "They are articulate, well-mannered, and involved in a lot of activities. The Michael Jordan Foundation came in and was impressed with our students. The foundation saw that there were things already going on in our school that they could build upon. We were very lucky that he selected Hartigan.

"The foundation and a committee of our teachers, students, and parents came up with incentives for academic achievement, and students with perfect attendance. Students receive recognition breakfasts with the principal, ribbons, buttons, and field trips. The foundation also wanted to see a school newspaper developed and published twice a year. Michael donated $10,000 as the initial investment in the program.

"The foundation also gave us a wonderful sign that hangs in our lobby. It says, 'The Michael Jordan Foundation Welcomes You Back to School.' It was originally put up during a spring break when the students were away. Now we use the sign to mean: Here is The Michael Jordan Foundation welcoming you back to school *each and every day*.

"We're also using Michael and the Bulls to teach math and geography, and to promote reading. The students follow the Bulls, and we study the team's statistics. We work with percentages and compare the Bulls' record to that of other teams. We use the team's travels to study geography based on where the team is playing.

"Michael is a hero to most of the children here, to most of the children in Chicago, and across the United States," Betty Greer says. "To have someone as important and as renowned as Michael Jordan adopt our school has caused the students to have greater self-esteem and become more involved in meeting the program's goals for attendance and scholarship. Michael is such a positive role model. Here is a young black male who shows by his own behavior, not only skill in terms of basketball, but also in promoting the values of education, staying in school, and clean living. He says, 'Stay away from drugs and drinking,' and he embodies the ideals we'd like to have for all our young people."

Education has been a major focus of The Michael Jordan Foundation. In addition to the foundation's work in Chicago, Michael has also been an active supporter of the United Negro College Fund.

As a college graduate, Michael is a firm believer that education holds the key to a person's success. Despite his sports success, Michael credits his education as being a crucial building block in his career.

"School and education have been a tremendous support to me, especially in my business management," Michael says. "Besides, I'll always have my education to fall back on if I decide on a career change."

The idea of Michael making a career change might have seemed farfetched as the Bulls entered the final month of the 1991–92 season. The team won eight of its last eleven games and Michael scored more than 40 points in five of those games. The Bulls ended the season with a 108–100 win over Detroit. As the game ended, Scottie Pippen, who had scored 28 points, shook hands with Detroit's John Salley.

"See you in the playoffs," Pippen predicted. "And this time it will be different," the Chicago forward promised.

The Bulls had their best season yet with 61 wins and 21 losses, finishing first in the Eastern Conference. Michael led the league in scoring, for the fifth season in a row, with a 31.5-point average.

Now it was on to the 1991 playoffs. Michael's and the Bulls' dream of winning their first championship was a little bit closer to coming true.

13
Showdowns and Shoot-outs

The Bulls made short work of the New York Knicks in the first round of the playoffs. The Bulls demolished the Knicks in the first game, beating them by 41 points, 126–85. Chicago went on to sweep the series.

The Bulls showed what a well-rounded team they had become as they easily won their first two playoff games against the Philadelphia 76ers. Bill Cartwright hit for 12 points in the first quarter of Game 1 and made mincemeat of the Sixers' center, seven-foot-seven-inch Manute Bol. Scottie Pippen and Michael combined for 53 points as the Bulls charged to a 105–92 win. Two nights later, they beat the Sixers again.

Michael had a spectacular 24-point second half in Game 3, but was matched by the hot-shooting Hersey Hawkins. With one minute left, the Bulls led 97–95. Michael played tight defense on Hawkins, determined that the Philadelphia guard would not burn the Bulls with a game-winning three-point shot. There were ten seconds left on the clock when Charles Barkley saw an opening and drove toward the basket. Michael, afraid Barkley would score, moved into the lane to stop the Sixer star. Barkley flipped the ball back to Hawkins who sank a long three-point jump shot. The 76ers took the lead and won the game. Michael had scored 46 points, but blamed the loss on himself since his man had scored the game-winning basket.

Jordan, Pippen, and Grant all topped the 20-point mark in a well-rounded scoring effort as Chicago coasted to a 101–85 win in Game 4. Scottie Pippen was red-hot in Game 5, shooting 13 for 14 before leaving the game in foul trouble. Suddenly, Chicago's 13-point lead evaporated. Michael went into high gear, scoring 12 points in the final three minutes. The Bulls won the game 100–95, and the series.

Michael had collected 38 points and 19 rebounds in the game. He was pleased, not only with his stats, but by the Bulls' well-rounded scoring attack.

"Things have changed," he told reporters after the game. "A few guys have emerged, a few guys have matured and we're a team now."

The Bulls felt the momentum was with them now. But they would need more than momentum to shut down Detroit, their next opponent. Detroit had eliminated the Bulls from the playoffs for three straight years. The Bulls were eager to reverse the trend.

These Pistons were hampered by injuries. Isiah

Thomas had hurt his wrist, foot, and hamstring. James Edwards was suffering from back problems, and Joe Dumars was plagued with tendinitis in both knees. Detroit still had Dennis Rodman, Bill Laimbeer (who'd bullied the Bulls year after year), Vinnie Johnson, and Mark Aguirre. There was no shortage of talent in the Pistons' lineup.

The Bulls roared to an early lead in Game 1, establishing a comfortable 20–8 lead in the first quarter. Detroit played their usual rough game, pushing and shoving the Bulls, especially Michael. But the Bulls refused to be intimidated.

Chicago was ahead in the third period when Jackson took out all but one starter, Horace Grant, and put in reserves Craig Hodges, Will Perdue, B.J. Armstrong, and Cliff Levingston. The second unit not only held the lead but lengthened it to 81–72. The final score read 94–83. Michael had scored just 22 points. The rest of the Bulls had come through. Pippen had produced 18 points, and Cartwright 16; and the reserves chipped in 30!

"I had a bad game," Michael said, "and we still won. I think that shows the maturity of our team. I think this shows them we've got a team instead of a one-man situation."

After the game, Michael was named the NBA Most Valuable Player. With his teammates standing next to him, Michael felt a surge of pride as the Chicago Stadium crowd rose in unison to give him a deafening ovation. While the honor gave him great satisfaction, Michael had other things on his mind.

"Winning the award is great and I graciously

accept it on behalf of my family, my teammates, and the Chicago Bulls organization. But I'd much rather be standing here in June, waiting to receive a championship ring. I'm envious of the Detroit Pistons, the Los Angeles Lakers, the Boston Celtics, teams that have celebrated winning championships. That's something I badly want. It's the driving force for me right now."

Michael also gave credit to his teammates. "My teammates deserve most of the credit for my winning the MVP award. By our winning 61 games this year and becoming a stronger championship contender, it brought attention to the year I was having."

Michael's knees were hurting. Over the years, he'd developed painful tendinitis in his left knee. Despite his sore knees, Michael scored 35 points as the Bulls won the second game, 105–97, in front of a boisterous home-team crowd.

The series then moved to Detroit's home court. The Bulls hadn't won a single playoff game there since the Pistons opened the Palace in 1988. The Bulls broke their unlucky streak with a 113–107 win. The Bulls now had a 3–0 lead in the series.

Detroit tried to counter the Bulls' swarming offense with physical force in the fourth game. In the first period, John Paxson drove to the basket, only to be slammed out of bounds by Bill Laimbeer. Paxson responded with an amazing 10-point tear, pumping in three straight jumpers and four foul shots to give the Bulls an early lead. Chicago kept pouring in the points, and the Bulls won 115–94. The Bulls had swept the series. They were ecstatic. Some of the Pistons congratulated the Bulls, but others sulked and skulked off the court, refusing to shake hands.

"We surprised a lot of people and we surprised ourselves," Michael said after the game. "We didn't feel we could sweep this team but we knew we could beat them. We had to accept every beating, and every elbow they gave us, and stay focused on our goal."

The key to the victory had been Scottie Pippen. He had averaged 22 points per game, but more important, he had taken the pressure off Michael Jordan. The Pistons had tried to double-team and harass Michael the entire series. Thanks to Pippen's performance, the Bulls had discovered the secret to overturning The Jordan Rules. It was simple — find a dependable second shooter when Jordan was covered.

The Bulls now were headed to the NBA Finals. It was a joyful moment for Michael, his teammates, and the long-suffering Chicago fans. The only thing that stood in the way of winning the championship was the Los Angeles Lakers. The Lakers were a powerhouse. They had made it to the NBA Finals nine times since 1980 and had won the championship five times.

The Finals were billed as "The Show of Shows;" "Magic versus Michael." Two of basketball's best, Michael Jordan and Magic Johnson, were set to square off in what promised to be the ultimate showdown and shoot-out. Michael was the game's leading scorer, Magic the NBA's all-time assist leader. Many writers said Magic's team play had been the key to the Lakers' success. Michael Jordan, they said, may have more raw physical abilities, but his talents had never taken the Bulls to the top. The charge only made Michael more determined to win.

The night before his first championship series, Michael couldn't sleep. He went to bed around 12:30 A.M., but tossed and turned most of the night. When he woke up at 7:30, Michael was still nervous. To give him a boost, he put on a Stevie Wonder compact disc and listened to the song, "Fun Day," over and over again. He listened to it on his car CD player on the way to Chicago Stadium, telling himself, "This is gonna be a fun day."

Chicago Stadium has a reputation as one of the noisiest basketball arenas in the NBA. "There is never a quiet moment in Chicago Stadium," Michael once said. Former Bulls' coach Stan Albeck described the place as a "madhouse." The noise level was thunderous as the Bulls and Lakers took the court for the first game of the best-of-seven series. The match turned into a seesaw battle. In the third period, Magic, James Worthy, and Sam Perkins began pouring in points, giving the Lakers a 75–68 lead. Michael was on his way to a 36-point game, but, except for Scottie Pippen, the rest of the Bulls were cold. Michael kept Chicago in the game, and with less than 30 seconds left, the Bulls pulled ahead 91–89.

Magic spotted Sam Perkins open, just beyond the three-point line. He fired the ball to Perkins, who connected. The Lakers led by one. Fans began anxiously counting down the game's final 10 seconds. With 4 seconds remaining, the Bulls fed the ball to Michael who shot from 18 feet. It was the kind of buzzer-beating shot that Michael had made many times in clutch situations. The ball hit the rim and, for a moment, it seemed as if it would fall in. Then it bounced out, ensuring the Lakers' victory. It was plain from the look on his face that Michael was disgusted with himself.

"We had every opportunity to win," Michael said in the locker room. "But I missed my two last shots."

Michael bounced back with 33 points in Game 2, but he also got plenty of help from his teammates. Grant and Pippen each had 20 points, and John Paxson hit all eight of his shots for 16 points. The game turned into a rout as the Bulls won 107–86.

Lakers fans jammed the Forum, Los Angeles' home court, for Game 3. Local newspapers predicted the Bulls would be tamed on the Lakers' turf. While Michael struggled and missed 17 of 28 shots, Magic dissected the Bulls' defense like a surgeon. The Lakers had a 92–90 lead with 5 seconds left. Two seconds later, Michael launched a 14-foot jump shot. It was good and it tied the game. In the final seconds, the Lakers fed the ball to their big man, seven-foot-one-inch Vlade Divac. Before the L.A. center could get off a game-winning shot, Michael slapped the ball out of his hands. The game went into overtime, where Michael and Horace Grant led the Bulls to victory, 104–96. The Bulls now led the series two games to one.

Whatever home-court advantage the Lakers might have enjoyed disappeared, as injuries took their toll on the Los Angeles' lineup. James Worthy had a sprained ankle, and Byron Scott was playing with a sore shoulder. Michael, playing with a bruised toe, scored 28 points and had 13 assists. Many of those assists went to John Paxson, who had 15 points. The Bulls coasted to a 97–82 victory. All the Bulls needed now was one more victory.

The Lakers were still missing Worthy and Scott in Game 5. Behind strong shooting from Sam Perkins, substitute Elden Campbell, and Magic, who had 20 assists, the Lakers took the lead 93–90 in the final minutes of the fourth quarter. Moments later, Scottie Pippen nailed a three-pointer to tie the game.

Then, the John Paxson show began. Paxson took three long jump shots, made them all, then scored again on a driving lay-up. But Sam Perkins retaliated with his own eight-point surge, and pulled the Lakers within two, 103–101.

There was less than a minute left. Michael got the ball and drove downcourt. He cut to the basket, and Magic, Divac, and Perkins all moved to stop him. Michael, having drawn the Lakers' defense, spun and whirled. He knew Paxson was open right behind him. Without looking, he whipped a pass directly to his rear. Paxson caught the ball and shot. It was good. It was Paxson's fifth basket in four minutes, and it put the game away. It was a fitting symbol of how Michael and the Bulls had learned to work together. The Bulls went on to win the game and the NBA championship.

After the game, fans flooded the court. Magic Johnson made his way through the crowd to Michael.

"You proved everyone wrong," Magic told Michael. "You're a winner as well as a great basketball player."

In the Bulls' locker room, NBA commissioner David Stern presented the team with the gold championship trophy. Emotion flooded over Michael and he felt his knees get weak. His father, mother, and wife at his side, Michael wept unashamedly. The Bulls were pouring champagne all over each other, but Michael hardly noticed the spray soaking his skin. In an instant, all the criticisms that Michael was not a championship-caliber player, or that he had not elevated his teammates' level of play, disappeared. Someone handed Michael the trophy, and he held it like a precious child, feeling the cool metal on his face.

"I never thought I'd be this emotional, but I don't mind. This is a great feeling, a great situation to be emotional," he said, the tears still visible on his cheeks.

"It means so much. When I first got to Chicago, we started at the bottom and every year we worked harder and harder till we got to the top. I've appreciated so much in my life, from my family, from my kids, everything. But this is the most proud day I've ever had.

"No one can ever take this away from me," Michael told the press, his voice cracking with emotion. "This has been a seven-year struggle for me.

I should get rid of the stigma of being a one-man team. We have players surrounding myself that make us an effective basketball team. Now my teammates have stepped up and the stigma is removed. I don't know if I'll ever have this same feeling again."

Michael was named the league's Most Valuable Player and the MVP for the NBA Finals. Michael also gave something back to his teammates. After winning the championship, the Walt Disney Company had offered Michael $100,000 to make a commercial for Disney World. Michael agreed to do it only if the entire starting five of the Bulls were included. Michael asked that the money be split five ways, too. It was a fitting gesture of Michael's respect and gratitude toward his teammates.

The Bulls flew into Chicago's O'Hare Airport the next day. When the Bulls' plane landed, hundreds of fans were waiting behind the fence along the runway to greet the conquering heroes. Jet engines roared as planes landed and took off, but all the Bulls could hear were the cheers from the fans. Michael, looking dapper in a brown suit and shades, gave high fives to the fans who reached through the fence. Michael smiled as fans clamored to touch his fingertips. When Michael returned to his home in suburban Chicago, more than one hundred fans were there to greet him with signs, balloons, and banners. Michael joked that if his address had ever been a secret, it surely wasn't one anymore.

Later, there was a parade honoring the Bulls and a huge rally at Chicago's Grant Park. There were more than 500,000 fans, including kids, parents holding newborn babies, and grandparents. Some Chicagoans had waited twenty-five years for this moment. As the warm summer breezes blew off nearby Lake Michigan, Michael held the championship trophy aloft, his son Jeffrey by his side. As the fans cheered, Michael took the microphone.

"It's been a struggle, seven long years," he said. "We started from the bottom and it was hard working our way to the top. But we did it."

Chicago may have had the nickname "Second City" (after New York City), but in pro basketball, it was now number one.

14
Unbeata-Bulls

Michael kept his championship ring on his dresser during the entire 1991–92 season. He kept it there as a reminder of the championship season and as a challenge to do it again. Michael had proven he was a champion, and with that achievement behind him he could concentrate on his game more than ever.

James Jordan had made a prediction following the 1991 season. "Now that he's gotten over the burden of winning a championship, Michael can play a lot more relaxed. Totally relaxed, and that's a scary situation."

Following a pregame ceremony in which the Bulls' championship banner was unfurled in Chicago Stadium, the Bulls took on the Philadelphia 76ers in the first game of the 1991–92 season. The Bulls were totally psyched and they roared to a 31-point lead in the second half. They beat the Sixers by a comfortable 110–90 margin behind Michael's 26 points and Scottie Pippen's 23.

Michael had three 40-plus point games in a row, but the Bulls lost two of those games. The Bulls took on the Celtics in Boston Garden in the fourth game of the season. It was the Celtics' five-hundredth sellout. Michael and the Bulls spoiled the party by whipping Boston 132–113 behind Michael's 44-point performance.

By their seventh game, the Bulls had moved into first place in the Central Division. They would remain there for the rest of the season, despite the fact that every team wanted to beat them more than ever before.

"Every team is playing us really tough because we're the defending champs. We're the guys to beat," Michael said. "I think the pressure is on us to play our best game every night. Obviously we want to repeat as the NBA champions."

The Bulls quickly ran off a streak of fourteen victories. Michael was already the NBA's leading scorer, but the Bulls' victories were driven by a balanced team effort that saw even reserve players like Stacy King and B.J. Armstrong scoring in double figures when they got enough playing time.

Michael's defensive skills were also helping win games. In a game against the Golden State Warriors, Michael guarded the high-scoring Chris Mullin. Michael held Mullin to 2 points in the first half, and the Bulls went on to win 112–108.

"It's no secret about Michael as a defensive player," Mullin said after the game. "He makes it tough to get open. He's the best there is defensively."

By mid-January, Chicago had surged to a 31–5

record, the best start in the team's history. Scottie Pippen was averaging more than 20 points a game. He had become one of the NBA's best players, one who could not only score, but pull down rebounds and play excellent defense. The on-court chemistry he and Michael had developed gave the Bulls a one-two scoring punch unmatched by any other NBA team.

Michael had always encouraged Pippen, and he described him as the best player he'd played with in his eight-year NBA career. "In some ways," Michael noted, "it's like looking in a mirror. He doesn't want to play at just one end of the court either. You don't always see that at this level. He's very dedicated."

"I've learned a lot from Michael," Pippen responded. "It took some adjusting, but he's very easy to play with. I know his style and he knows mine."

Chicago had become, as one sportswriter nicknamed them, "The Unbeata-Bulls." In early March, the Bulls became the first NBA team to clinch a playoff spot. Still, they didn't let up. They handed the Celtics their worst loss of the year, a 119–85 shellacking. To Michael and the Bulls, every game was a prelude to the playoffs.

"We want to send as many messages as we can before the playoffs. We don't want teams thinking they can beat us," Michael declared.

The Bulls ended the season with a 67–15 record, the best finish in the team's history. Michael led the league in scoring for the sixth time, just one less time than the record-holder Wilt Chamberlain.

Michael's fame, also, had reached greater heights. He signed a multimillion dollar deal with Gatorade, and saw his face and name on products ranging from chewing gum to cereal. Michael appeared in a steady stream of commercials, including a hilarious Nike one in which he teamed up with Bugs Bunny for "Hare Jordan" sneakers. He even became a Saturday morning cartoon character in a show called *Pro Stars*.

Estimates of Michael's earnings from endorsements from companies like Nike, Quaker Oats, and Hanes ranged from $10 to $15 million per year. In a marketing survey of advertising agencies, Michael was named the number-one most-wanted spokesman for products, topping Arnold Palmer, Joe Montana, and Wayne Gretzky.

Michael's business interests are varied and extensive, and he has involved his family in many of them. For example, both Larry and Roslyn work in and manage several Flight 23 by Jordan shops that sell Air Jordan sporting goods and sportswear. Michael's mother and father are also very involved in the stores.

Despite his wealth, Michael remains committed, through his foundation, to giving something back to those less fortunate. As Michael's fame grew over the years, he began to receive more and more letters from sick and terminally ill children, asking him to write or visit them. By the start of the 1992 season, Michael was receiving more than 1500 letters a year. Michael obliged as many children as he could, inviting many of them to be his guests at games up to seventy times a season.

Michael has also befriended burn victims and has been a big supporter of the Ronald McDonald Houses. His presence at celebrity galas and charity golf tournaments has brought in hundreds of thousands of dollars for a variety of causes. It is no wonder that Bill Russell, the great Boston Celtic center, once told Deloris Jordan that Michael was an even better human being than he was a basketball player.

Few athletes have inspired young people the way Michael has. On countless playgrounds across the country, kids strive to emulate not only Michael's moves, but also his positive and winning attitude. Like it says in the Gatorade commercials, kids truly want "to be like Mike." Michael himself advises kids to go one better. "They should be better than Mike," he says.

Michael's fame has transcended the world of basketball. An incident that took place during a recent charity golf tournament showed the level of craziness that surrounds a man of Michael's stature. During a break, Michael ate an apple and tossed the core into the nearby woods. Suddenly, a dozen young fans ran under the ropes and raced to the trees. One boy found the apple core and held it up as if it were a prize. The other boys looked on enviously. Everywhere he goes, Michael is mobbed.

At times, especially during the 1991–92 season, Michael found the spotlight too much. It became difficult to maintain his privacy. Michael frequently retreated to his family and home in the Chicago suburbs which he has equipped with a six-hole basement putting green, pool tables, and a state-of-the-art entertainment center. Other times he sought refuge on the golf course or in the company of longtime friends, many of whom he has known since his younger days in North Carolina.

The Bulls' quest to repeat as NBA champs intensified in late April. The Miami Heat, who had finished sixteenth in the NBA standings, had the bad luck to face the Bulls in the first round of the playoffs. Michael turned off the Heat with a 46-point performance in the first game and 56 points in the third game. The Bulls swept the three-game series. Michael's three-game scoring total against Miami was 135 points, topping his 1986 record of 131.

Miami center Rony Seikaly described Michael's scoring power in explosive terms. "He's like a hand grenade without the pin."

The odds were heavily against the New York Knicks, who faced Chicago in the Eastern Conference semifinals, a best-of-seven series. The Knicks had overpowered the Pistons in the previous round with their aggressive defense, giving Detroit a taste of their own medicine. However, the Knicks had lost fourteen consecutive games against the Bulls, and seventeen straight at Chicago Stadium, the site of the first game. No one thought the Knicks had a chance, and many sportswriters predicted a Bulls' sweep.

141

As a stunned Chicago Stadium crowd watched, New York shocked the Bulls and the sports world by taking the first game 94–89. With Scottie Pippen plagued by a sore ankle, Patrick Ewing burned Chicago's defense, scoring a game-high 34 points. "One game doesn't make a series," Michael promised. Coming back to win, however, was "going to take a lot of work," Michael admitted. He had no idea just how hard the Knicks were going to make him work.

The Knicks' tough defense forced the Bulls to work for every shot. The Bulls evened the series in Game 2 as B.J. Armstrong's late-game baskets and Michael's 27 points brought Chicago the victory. Things got really rough in Game 3. Michael got hit in the face by the "X-Man," Xavier McDaniel, and had a bloody nose for the final minutes of the game. Michael still scored 32 and the Bulls won 94–86.

Michael made the news that night, not for his scoring, but because of the soaring sky-high dunk he missed. In the second quarter, Scottie Pippen fired a pass to Michael who had broken downcourt. With no one to stop him, Michael took off and pumped a ferocious windmill slam at the basket. Michael jammed the ball so hard that it not only missed, but bounced off the back of the rim and landed 45 feet away. The miss was shown in instant replay three times!

"I was too intense. I was trying to take the rim down, but I just overpowered it and it came out," Michael said with a smile after the game. Even when Michael missed, he did it spectacularly.

When the Knicks won Game 4 to tie the series at two games each, some sportswriters began to wonder if Chicago had what it takes to win the NBA title again. The Knicks seemed a lot hungrier than the Bulls. Chicago, especially Scottie Pippen, seemed intimidated by the Knicks' ferocious defense. The Bulls had averaged nearly 110 points a game during the season. The Knicks had cut that by 21 points, holding the Bulls to less than 89 points per game so far. However, New York couldn't stop Michael. Despite a twisted ankle, Michael outscored everyone with 29 points. He also took most of the knocks from the Knicks' defense.

"There were a lot of arms and elbows, but it is nothing I haven't seen before," Michael said calmly after the game.

Before the next game, Michael declared he would not be intimidated by the Knicks' tough tactics. "The lane doesn't belong to anyone. Even if I'm going to get knocked down, I'm going to the hole," he promised.

Michael was determined not to let the Knicks get the better of the Bulls. Goaded on by a loud crowd at Chicago Stadium, Chicago won the fifth game as Michael scored 37 points, including 26 in the second half. Just as Michael's teammate, B.J. Armstrong, had helped the Bulls win Game 2, John Paxson ignited the Bulls' offense with seven straight points in the fourth quarter to help put the game out of New York's reach.

The Knicks bounced back two nights later in New York. As 20,000 towel-twirling fans taunted the Bulls, Patrick Ewing and three-point-shot specialist John Starks both scored 27 points and Xavier McDaniel chipped in 24 to lead the New York Knicks to a 100–86 victory. The Knicks' defense was flawless in the fourth quarter as they held Chicago scoreless for six straight minutes. Delirious New York fans poured out onto the streets surrounding Madison Square Garden, celebrating and predicting the Bulls' burial in the final and deciding seventh game in Chicago Stadium. No one had forgotten how the Bulls swept the Knicks in the 1991 playoffs or how Michael Jordan eliminated them with two last-second foul shots in 1989. The Knicks were ready for revenge.

"We're going to be bringing our black suits," New York guard Mark Jackson promised, "for a funeral."

Michael admitted he felt tired and mentally drained after the game. Pro basketball — with its constant running and jumping — is one of the most physically demanding sports. The regular season consists of six months of back-to-back games, and constant travel and training. The playoffs are even more grueling. The pace had been and would continue to be exhausting. However, after a day of rest, Michael felt rejuvenated and ready for the final and deciding game.

Michael spent the morning before the game with his father. He and James debated how Michael should play — cautiously or aggressively. James had no doubts. He reminded Michael that while it was good to get the other Bulls involved, this was an all-important seventh game. "Whether everyone is in it or not," James told his son, "you've just got to leave all of yourself on the court."

The funeral Mark Jackson had predicted turned out to be New York's. The Bulls buried the Knicks with a massive 110–81 rout. The game belonged to Michael who scored 29 in the first half and 42 in the game. He hit outside jumpers, tossed in reverse lay-ups over Patrick Ewing, and was a whirling defensive dervish. Horace Grant played a key role in the victory, hauling down rebounds and blocking shots, but it was Michael's determination and scoring power that carried the day.

"Michael rose to the occasion as he usually does in situations like this," Phil Jackson declared.

While the Knicks had lost the series, they'd won the Bulls' respect for taking the series to seven games. They'd also taught Michael and the Bulls not to be overconfident.

"New York deserves credit," Michael said. "They woke us up. We walked into the series thinking it would be a sweep, but it went seven. It was like a slap in the face. This hardened us for the next series."

The Eastern Conference finals pitted the Cavaliers against Chicago. Thanks to Mark Price, the best foul shooter in the league, seven-foot Brad Daugherty, one of the NBA's best passing and scoring centers, and shot-blocking specialist Larry Nance, the Cavs had compiled the second best record in the league.

Michael was named the NBA MVP the day before the series began. It was his third MVP award and his second in a row. "I want to thank my teammates and family for helping me stay strong to stay on top of our game," he said proudly. Michael was also named to the NBA's All-Defense team.

After the hard-hitting tactics of the Knicks, the Bulls found the Cavs easier to handle — at first. Chicago cruised to an easy win in the first game and the Chicago press compared the Cavs to marshmallows and cream puffs.

"This series is going to get tougher," promised Cleveland's coach Lenny Wilkens. He was right. The Cavs handed Chicago its worst loss of the season in the second game, beating the Bulls by 26 points. Michael, suffering from a sore throat and the flu, was held to just 20 points.

Cleveland proved to be a tough opponent and they took the series to six games. In that final game, Michael had a miserable first half, but Scottie Pippen and Horace Grant made up for it with their steady scoring. Michael, determined to make it to the championship round, came alive in the second half as he scored 23 points, including a dramatic three-point play that sealed the victory. However, Michael gave his teammates credit for the win.

"I want to give my teammates lots of credit," he said. "They really hung in there when I was shooting real bad."

The Bulls' opponent in the Finals were the Portland Trail Blazers. The Blazers hadn't won a championship since 1977. They had made it to the finals in 1990, but were defeated by Detroit. Now Portland was as hungry for a championship as the Bulls had been a year earlier.

Portland's star guard, Clyde "The Glide" Drexler, was considered the best all-around player in the NBA after Michael. In fact, he had finished second behind Michael in the voting for the NBA MVP. The championship series was billed as a showdown between the two superstar guards, and Michael relished the chance to take on a player of Clyde's caliber.

"I take it as another challenge," Michael said. "I'm a competitor and I need something to drive me. Every game this season I felt someone was trying to take something away from me personally, so that was my motivation to step onto the basketball court and compete. With all the hype about Clyde and myself, that's the competition I need to raise my game."

The afternoon before the first game, Michael was joined in a pregame workout by his friend Buzz Peterson, now the assistant basketball coach at North Carolina State. Michael and Buzz played H-O-R-S-E, a game whose goal is to hit outside shots from all over the court.

The long-distance shooting session must have helped Michael because he was deadly from the perimeter that night. Since Michael had made just 27 of 100 three-point shots during the season, Clyde Drexler gave Michael plenty of room from the outside. It was a mistake, and Michael took the opportunity to rewrite the record book. He hit 14 field goals, including 6 three-point shots in the first half, tying two NBA records. Michael ended up with 35 points in the first half, breaking Elgin Baylor's playoff record of 33. Michael finished with

39, as the Bulls romped to a 122–89 blowout.

"Michael could have been in the first balcony and made a shot," Horace Grant said with a laugh.

Michael, however, was wary of becoming over-confident. "That was just one game. One game doesn't make the Finals," he warned. Two nights later, the lesson was hammered home.

The Bulls had a 10-point lead with just over four minutes left in Game 2 when Clyde Drexler committed his sixth foul and had to leave the game. As the Chicago Stadium crowd and public address system serenaded him with the Ray Charles' song, "Hit the Road, Jack," it looked like a sure win for the Bulls. However, the Blazers made a dramatic comeback. With less than a minute left, Portland's seven-foot, 280-pound center Kevin Duckworth bulldozed his way to the basket and sank a jump shot to tie the game 97–97. In the final seconds, the Bulls got the ball to Michael. He let go a desperate jump shot, but it missed. The game went into overtime, and so did Portland's Danny Ainge. He went on a 9-point tear in the overtime to lead the Blazers to a 115–104 victory.

Chicago's defense pulled out all the stops in the third game, blocking shots, making steals, and forcing the Blazers to work hard for their shots. Clyde Drexler still managed to score 32, but Portland's hot shooting guard, Terry Porter, was held to 7, 15 less than his playoff average. Michael scored 26, while Pippen and Grant each added 18, but it was the team's defense that was responsible for Chicago's 94–84 win.

"Whenever we get our backs to the wall, we let

our defense take over. We made them make tough shots and battled them on the boards," Michael said.

However the Blazers made another dramatic comeback in Game 4. The Bulls led for most of the game, but Portland managed to hold Michael scoreless for 10 minutes in the fourth quarter. The Bulls were still ahead with 3 minutes to go in the game, but Chicago blew its lead again. Portland won 93–88, and the series was tied once more.

The same day, Michael had been voted the *Sporting News* Player of the Year by his fellow NBA players. He got 109 votes while the runner-up, Clyde Drexler, got 13. Still, the loss in Game 4 was a disappointment. Michael took his mind off the series with a game of golf prior to Game 5.

"Golf," he said, "is like medicine for my mind. It helps me relax."

Twice before — against the Knicks and the Cavaliers — the series had been tied at two games apiece, and each time the Bulls had won the fifth game. The Bulls charged to an early 17-point lead in the first half of Game 5, but got a terrible scare in the second period. Michael Jordan outmaneuvered a Portland double-team and took a fall-away jump shot from the corner. He missed, and his momentum caused him to fall into a crowd of photographers at courtside. When he got up, he was limping. He had tripped on a photographer's camera and sprained an ankle. After a minute of rest, Michael came back, hit a three-point jump shot and two free throws to boost the lead to 19. This time the lead held, and the Bulls beat the

Blazers 119–106. Michael, despite the sprained ankle, scored a series-high 46 points, while Scottie Pippen had his best game of the series, tossing in 24 points.

Michael's scoring may have won the game for the Bulls, but it was his inner strength that won the respect of the Blazers. "Michael is a special kind of player," said Portland forward Buck Williams after the game. "He showed that tonight. He wasn't going to be denied. He does what has to be done to win."

The action returned to Chicago Stadium for what the Bulls hoped would be the final game. The odds were heavily against the Blazers. No team had ever won the NBA crown by taking two straight games on their opponent's court. History was on the Bulls' side, but Michael wasn't taking anything for granted.

"We know how close we are, but the closer you are, the harder it is," he noted.

Portland pulled ahead early in Game 6. A 10-point burst by Michael in the second half narrowed Portland's lead to 50–44, but the Blazers were red-hot in the third period. When the third quarter ended, the Blazers led 79–64. Now history was against the Bulls. The largest margin an NBA team had ever overcome in the fourth quarter of a final game was 12. The Bulls were down by 15.

Coach Phil Jackson gave Michael a rest as the fourth quarter began. To the surprise of everyone in the packed stadium, he went with reserves B.J. Armstrong, Scott Williams, Bobby Hansen, and

Stacey King. The only member of the Bulls' starting lineup in the game was Scottie Pippen. As Michael sat on the bench cheering his teammates, the reserves and Pippen outscored the Blazers 14 to 2 to bring the Bulls back. Portland was ahead 83–78, when Michael returned to the game with just over 8 minutes left.

Pippen slipped past the Blazers' defense to sink a lay-up to make it 83–80. The crowd was now on their feet, sensing a comeback. In a split-second move, Michael stole the ball at midcourt and arched a floater over Clyde Drexler's arms. The shot was good. The Bulls were now within one.

After Terry Porter sank two foul shots to make the score 85–82, the Bulls brought the ball downcourt. With just two seconds left on the 24-second shot clock, Scottie Pippen launched a long three-point shot. It swished through the net to tie the score. The Chicago fans went berserk.

For the next few minutes, the two teams battled back and forth. With less than four minutes to go, Michael performed a lightning-fast steal and stuff move against Buck Williams. Williams had grabbed a rebound off a missed Chicago shot, but Michael slipped behind him and stole the ball right under the basket. Michael slammed in a two-handed dunk, and the Bulls took the lead 89–87.

After a Portland turnover, Michael got the ball again. He drove down the lane, stopped short, then let go a twisting fall-away jumper. It was good. A minute later, Michael slipped past the Blazers' defense and flew along the baseline to the basket. He tossed in a spinning shot off the backboard and the Bulls suddenly had a 95–91 lead. Portland fought back and scored again, but Michael had the last word. With 40 seconds left and Chicago ahead 95–93, Michael was fouled and went to the line for two shots. He had the chance to put the game out of Portland's reach, and he did just that. He sank both shots, and the Bulls won 97–93. It was the greatest comeback in the history of the NBA Finals, and Chicago Stadium erupted with cheers and screams. As the public address system blared Queen's, "We Are the Champions," Michael jumped up, pumping his fists in the air over and over.

Michael had again risen to the occasion, scoring 12 of the Bulls' final 19 points. The Bulls had won their second straight championship, joining the elite ranks of the three other great teams who had won back-to-back titles: the Celtics, Lakers, and Pistons.

Michael's individual achievements also had the mark of greatness. His scoring average against Portland was 35.8 points, the highest total of any winning player in Finals' history. Michael was named the MVP in the Finals. It marked the first time a player had won both the regular season MVP and the Finals MVP award two years in a row.

After the game, Michael praised his teammates, especially Scottie Pippen and the reserves. "Everybody contributed. These guys really carried us. It was a good team effort," he said happily.

Michael also felt an enormous sense of relief. Except for the year he broke his foot, the 1991–92 season had been Michael's toughest ever. His opponents had played him harder than ever before, and the pursuit of the championship had been the biggest challenge of his career. Never had the press and public eye been so focused on every aspect of Michael's life than it was in 1992.

In the locker room after the game, the Bulls received their second championship trophy. Michael, with his wife Juanita by his side, said, "It's so gratifying for me personally. I went through a lot of hard times this year, but I stayed strong. It was one of those years I matured and probably improved as a player. But also in life in general I matured quite a bit. I'm glad the year's over."

The fans in Chicago Stadium had refused to leave until the Bulls came out for a curtain call. Michael and the rest of the Bulls ran out onto the floor to a deafening ovation. They jumped on the scorer's table and did a victory dance to the delight of their fans. Michael held the trophy aloft in one hand, and with his other hand, held up three fingers. The gesture indicated that the Bulls were already thinking about the possibility of winning three straight championships.

Later Michael was asked about it. "We haven't focused on next year yet, but when it's time we will, and I think going for three in a row will give us that challenge we need," he said. "And you have to have challenges to play your best."

At a rally two days later, hundreds of thousands of Chicago Bulls' fans gathered in Grant Park to pay tribute to their team. Michael, clutching the championship trophy, thanked the fans and the Bulls' organization. "Thank God *they* drafted me instead of Portland," he said with a smile. The fans cheered in agreement.

15
Going for the Gold

Michael's 1992 basketball season did not end with the NBA Finals. He had been selected to play basketball for the United States team in the 1992 Olympic Games in Barcelona, Spain. For the first time, NBA players would be allowed to compete. The lineup of the U.S. team was awesome: Larry Bird, Magic Johnson, Karl Malone, Charles Barkley, Patrick Ewing, David Robinson, Scottie Pippen, John Stockton, Chris Mullin, Clyde Drexler, and one college star, Christian Laettner from Duke University. It would be the greatest basketball team ever assembled. No wonder the superstar-studded squad was nicknamed "The Dream Team."

For Michael, playing in the Olympics a second time was a tremendous thrill. "When I got the opportunity to play in the Olympics when I was in college, it was a dream come true. Now I get to do it twice. It's very rare that people get to do something of this stature twice."

While Michael — the competitor — was eager to take on the world's best basketball teams in the Summer Games, he was also looking forward to playing on the same team with his NBA rivals. "I know it's very competitive. It's us against the world. But it's also an opportunity to get to know many great athletes I normally compete against all year long and meet them in a social atmosphere."

After the NBA championship, Michael headed home to North Carolina for a three-day rest, then joined the Dream Team for pre-Olympic practices in San Diego. The team's first test was the Tournament of the Americas in Portland, Oregon. The tournament pitted teams from North and South America against each other and only the four top finishers would make it to the Olympics.

The Dream Team might as well have been named the Cream Team because they totally creamed the opposition. They beat Canada by 44 points, Panama by 60, and Cuba by 79! The 79-point difference was the largest margin of victory in 66 years of international competition. With the pressure of the NBA championship off his shoulders, Michael took a low profile role in the scoring department. His best game was against Canada where he scored 14 points and grabbed six rebounds in 22 minutes of play. With most of the attention focused on Magic Johnson and high-scoring Charles Barkley, Michael said he simply wanted to blend in with his teammates and was not at all worried about scoring. With the Dream Team's lineup he didn't have to be. "If I score, fine. If I don't, that's fine, too," he said.

The Dream Team beat Venezuela by 47 points, giving them the championship in the tournament. There was a two-week break before the Olympic Games were set to begin and Michael used the time to relax with family and friends, at home and on the golf course.

Michael looked rested and ready when he arrived at Newark Airport in New Jersey for his flight to Europe. He was greeted by a crowd of autograph-seeking fans who ran behind him as he hurried to make his plane. The Dream Team was flying to Monaco for its practice sessions because the tiny principality — nestled between France and Spain — is home to European royalty and famous stars. It was felt that the team would attract less attention with all the jet-set celebrities who lived there. Instead, the team was met by starstruck fans bedecked in Chicago Bulls' hats and T-shirts, and other NBA gear. Some clutched posters of Michael and Magic. The players were given a warm welcome — and a royal banquet — by Monaco's Prince Rainier.

Michael intended to relax and enjoy the trip. He had brought his golf clubs and took in a Sunday game on a local course. "It's like summer camp," he said, "except that I can't swim, so I'm not going near the pool."

In their final game before the Olympics in Barcelona, the Dream Team played an exhibition against France. With Prince Rainier and his son Prince Albert in the stands, the Dream Team coasted to a 111–71 win as the fans chanted Mi-

chael's and Magic's names. Michael scored 13 of
the USA's first 17 points, and 21 in the game. He
added several spectacular dunks and reverse lay-
ups to the Dream Team's amazing offensive show.
The crowd cheered louder for the Americans than
they did for the home team, France.

"It's a sign of respect, and they appreciate being
able to see us in person," Michael noted. "You
don't always understand the language, but you understand your name."

The toughest opponent the Dream Team faced
at first was itself. Breaking into two squads in practices, the Dream Team scrimmaged — Jordan,
Bird, Ewing, Pippen, and Malone on one side and
Magic, Mullin, Barkley, Laettner, and Robinson on
the other. After Magic's team went on a 14–2 tear,
Magic challenged Michael to "get into his game or
lose." Michael took over his squad's offense and hit
several three-point shots and hard-driving dunks.
In the end, Michael's team won 40–36.

Barcelona was primed for Dream Team mania.
Sitting high over a busy Barcelona square was a
huge Nike billboard that featured a seven-story
mural of Michael in a Bulls' uniform doing a high-
flying reverse lay-up. Hours before the Dream
Team arrived, fans, reporters, and TV camera
crews began gathering outside the Hotel Ambas-
sador. One of the fans was 15-year-old Javier Roig.
He wore a Bulls' hat, Michael Jordan T-shirt, red
and black sweats, and, of course, Air Jordan sneakers. Displaying a poster of Michael, the Spanish
teenager proclaimed, "This is my coach."

The crowd grew to 500 by evening. As police sirens wailed and TV lights illuminated the street, a bus pulled up. "USA Basketball is coming," fans yelled. Michael and his teammates were met by loud cheers and whistles. In press accounts, reporters compared the scene to a visit by rock music superstars.

The day before the Olympic Games began, the Dream Team held a press conference. A huge crowd of reporters from all over the world showed up. One of them took the microphone to ask Michael a question.

"You are so good," the journalist said. "Are you an extra-terrestrial?"

After he finished laughing, Michael responded, "No, I'm from Chicago."

Michael and his teammates might as well have been from another planet because they were certainly in a class by themselves. The Dream Team reigned in Spain. They crushed Angola 116–48 as Michael scored 10 and had eight steals. Croatia posed more of a threat. The Croatian team had an NBA star, Drazen Petrovic of the New Jersey Nets, and Toni Kukoc, one of the best players in Europe. As always, Michael responded to the challenge. Chewing gum, eyes intently focused on the action, Michael pulled off several lightning-fast steal-and-stuff moves that gave the United States an early lead. He ended up the game's leading scorer with 21 points and the team leader in steals with eight.

"We were really ready to play," Michael told reporters after the game. "We were very focused because it was supposed to be our toughest challenge."

After Magic Johnson strained his hamstring muscle, Michael took over the point-guard position for the game against Germany. He led the U.S. to a 111–68 win as he collected 14 points and 12 assists. "The man could play any position," coach Chuck Daly proclaimed.

In the next game, Brazil took an early lead but ended up losing 127–83. No Olympic basketball team had ever scored as many points in a game as the 127 the Dream Team produced against Brazil.

Michael was not only enjoying socializing with his fellow players, but he also appreciated the chance to play with — not against — basketball's best. "I've tried to show the coaches and the players what I can do other than scoring. The relationship with the players has been really more than I expected. It's been great."

Michael, suffering from the effects of a virus, had an off night against Spain, missing 11 of his 16 shots and collecting 11 points. However, the Dream Team still trounced the Spanish team 122–81. The hometown fans cheered the Americans anyway. After the game, Michael had an emotion-filled moment as he embraced the Spanish team's coach, Antonio Diaz-Miguel, the man who had called Michael "a rubber man" at the 1984 Games. After 27 years as the Spanish team's coach, Diaz-Miguel had announced he was quitting the job. Diaz-Miguel had been a frequent visitor to Chapel

Hill and other American universities over the years and he and Michael had become friends. Michael wished Diaz-Miguel luck as he hugged the Spaniard at center court.

The Dream Team continued its winning ways against Puerto Rico and Lithuania. Lithuania was supposed to be a tough team, but as expected, the Dream Team dominated the game from the opening tap. Michael was at his best, hitting outside jumpers, pulling off amazing inside moves for dunks, making steals, and playing ferocious defense. He and Magic sparked a 20–0 run against the Lithuanians in the first half, and by the game's end the Dream Team had crushed them by a 51-point margin, 127–76. Michael was the game's high scorer with 21 points.

"This team becomes real scary in terms of what we can do whenever we feel like we're being challenged," Michael said after the game. Interestingly enough, the Lithuanians, just like all the other teams, were less intimidated by the Americans than they were thrilled to be on the same court as the Dream Team. After the games, many of them clamored to have their picture taken with Michael, Magic, and the others.

The gold medal game was a rematch against the Croatian team. To no one's surprise, the United States won 117–85. Michael went all out, as he always does when the stakes are high. With 22 points, he was again the team's top scorer. He had also shown throughout the games that even compared to the rest of the Dream Team, he was the best of the best. He was the only player to start all the games. For the second time, Michael had won an Olympic gold medal.

"He's the greatest, the best without doubt," Magic Johnson declared. "He can do whatever he wants, when he wants, however he wants."

Coach Chuck Daly agreed. "It's not even close. Whenever he wanted to, he could just take over."

16
Triumph and Tragedy

In the fall of 1992, Michael returned to the Bulls a little worse for wear. While the Olympics had been an exhilarating experience, it had also been an exhausting one for Michael. Neither he nor Scottie Pippen had a chance to relax before the new season got underway. "After playing all the way into June, then all summer with the Olympic team," Michael commented, "I didn't want to see the ball. It was like 'Hey, I'm right back here already?'"

As the 1992–93 season began, Michael knew the Bulls faced a huge challenge, their biggest yet. Only two teams, the Minnesota Lakers and the Boston Celtics, had won three straight championships. Magic Johnson, who had won five championship rings, had told Michael before the 1992–93 season, "If the Bulls think winning two in a row was hard, they'll find out that winning three in a row will be the hardest thing they'll ever do."

Michael faced a personal challenge as well. Taking a team to the NBA title was the mark of a great player. Doing it three times in a row was extraordinary. "Magic couldn't do it and Bird couldn't do it and Isiah couldn't do it," Michael reminded reporters, adding, "It's the thing that really drives me now."

Michael started strong, scoring 29 in the Bulls' season opener, a 101–96 win against Cleveland. He pumped in 35 points in a 100–99 loss to Atlanta, then scored 37 points in a dramatic overtime victory against the Pistons. It was Michael's 30-foot three-point shot that gave the Bulls the 98–96 victory in that game.

Karl Malone of the Utah Jazz and Dominique "Human Highlight Film" Wilkins of the Hawks, took the number one and number two spots in scoring during the first weeks of the 1992–93 season; then Michael got red-hot. In the week before Thanksgiving, he scored 40 points against the Suns in a 128–111 win, and 49 points to beat the Warriors 101–92. After those games, he took over the top scoring spot and held it for the rest of the season.

In late November, the Knicks routed the Bulls, 112–75. Michael sprained his foot in the first quarter and missed nine minutes of the game. The 75 points the Bulls scored were the fewest they'd ever scored against the Knicks. New York's performance was a stinging reminder not to take them for granted in the battle for the Eastern Conference title.

A month later, on the day after Christmas, Michael paid the Knicks back. He scored 42 points to lead the Bulls to a come-from-behind 89–77 victory. "They better respect us," Michael warned.

In a January game against the Milwaukee Bucks, the Bulls were on their way to a 120–95 blowout when Michael sank a three-point shot with just over five minutes left in the game. The shot put Michael's career total points at the 20,000 mark, making him the 18th player to reach that milestone. When he left the game moments later, the hometown crowd of 20,000 gave Michael a rousing standing ovation. Michael had reached 20,000 points in just 620 games, second only to Wilt Chamberlain, who did it in 499 games.

Michael was again named a starter for the Eastern Conference All-Star team in 1993. In the All-Star game in February, Michael was guarded by the Phoenix Suns' Dan Majerle, a dangerous three-point shooter and a defensive ace as well. The game went into overtime, where Majerle's tough defense held Michael to five points. Despite Michael's game total of 30 points, the East lost, 135–132. After the game, Majerle was asked about playing defense against the game's best player. "What I try to do is make him take a shot he's not really comfortable with, keep him outside and a hand in his face," Majerle explained. "And it's not like you can count on that working."

Majerle's team, the Suns, were having an outstanding year, thanks to players like Majerle, Kevin Johnson, and Charles Barkley. Many people predicted that the Jordan–Majerle All-Star-game match-up was a sneak preview of the soon-to-come NBA Finals.

By the end of the season, the predictions appeared close to coming true. The Suns had put together the best record in basketball with 62 wins and 20 losses. The Bulls finished second in the Eastern Conference behind the Knicks and qualified easily for the playoffs. Michael finished the season with an average of 32.6 points, good enough to lead the league and tie Wilt Chamberlain's record of seven straight scoring titles.

The Bulls' first-round playoff opponent was Atlanta. Despite the presence of Dominique Wilkins, the Bulls grounded the Hawks in three straight.

The Bulls took on the Cavaliers in the next round of the playoffs, winning the first two games easily. Late in Game 2, Michael sprained a ligament in the wrist of his shooting hand. Michael shot poorly in the first half of the third game, but came roaring back to finish with 32 points to sink the Cavs again.

By the fourth quarter of Game 4, the Bulls appeared to be on the brink of a second straight sweep. The score stood 101–101 with just seconds left, and Michael had the ball. Cleveland's Gerald Wilkins' defense was skintight and he managed to knock the ball loose for a split second, but Michael recovered the ball and his balance. With less than a second showing on the clock, and with Wilkins' hand in his face, Michael launched an 18-foot fallaway jump shot. Michael buried it, winning the game, the series, and sinking the Cavs' playoff hopes once again. Cleveland sportswriters dubbed Michael's missile the "Son of the Shot," referring to the buzzer-beater he sank against Craig Ehlo in the 1989 playoffs.

The Knicks were eager for another shot with

166

Chicago. Fans in the Big Apple and Coach Pat Riley were also hungry for a title — and they believed the Knicks' time had come. Michael felt otherwise. "Deep in our hearts," he said, "we know we can beat this team."

The Knicks didn't share Michael's opinion. In a hard-fought physical contest, the Knicks won Game 1 of the Eastern Conference finals, 98–90. Patrick Ewing scored 25 points and pulled down 17 rebounds and John Starks chipped in 25 points, and "held" Michael to a below-average 27. "You don't stop Michael Jordan. That's impossible," said Starks. "All you try to do is contain Michael Jordan."

The night before Game 2, Michael and his father traveled to Atlantic City. While Michael scored 36 in Game 2 the next day, his shooting and timing seemed to be off, and the Bulls lost again, 96–91. The press speculated that Michael's late-night trip had tired him out and adversely affected his game. Michael was growing increasingly frustrated with the nonstop media attention. Every move he made seemed to be scrutinized by the media, and what little privacy he once had was gone. For several days after, Michael stopped talking to the press.

Michael continued to struggle in Game 3, missing 15 of 18 shots from the field but making 16 of 17 foul shots for a total of 22 points. The rest of the Bulls stepped up their efforts, however, and scored enough to win by 20 points, 103–83.

Michael's mood was grim when Game 4 began in Chicago. Michael was still not talking to the media and let his game speak for him. He tossed up three-point shots that hit nothing but the net, and drove to the basket for some thunderous slam-dunks. He scored 18 points in the third quarter and ended the game with 54 points total. Michael's performance was "spectacular," said teammate Bill Cartwright. "This is something you only see a few times a year."

Michael contributed a triple double in Game 5 with 29 points, 14 assists, and 10 rebounds. Throughout the game, Michael was faced with a double-team defense. When he was, he dished the ball off to teammates like Scottie Pippen, who delivered 28 points of his own. Partly as a result of Michael's many assists, the Bulls won the match, 97–94. With the series now standing at 3–2 in favor of Chicago, the momentum had shifted. In Game 6, Michael's 25 points, plus the steady shooting of Scottie Pippen and John Paxson, gave the Bulls the win, 96–88, and the Knicks were again knocked out.

"It's all about making history now," Michael said as Game 1 of the 1993 NBA Finals against Phoenix began. The Suns had put together the best record in basketball in 1992–93, and Charles Barkley had been named the regular-season MVP. Barkley called the Suns "the team of destiny." He and his teammates were psyched to win a title.

In the first game, the Bulls won 100–92 as Michael racked up 31 points. After the game, reports began to circulate that Michael would retire "soon" because he was fed up with all the media attention and lack of privacy in his off-court life.

"I did say soon," he told the press, "but no one knows what soon is. Soon can be next year, in two years." Michael also wished to spend more time with his family, especially since the birth of his daughter, Jasmine, earlier in the year.

The Bulls won again in Phoenix in Game 2, and the Suns' hopes began to dim. "We're in a big hole now and we're in the right state for holes. We'd fit into the Grand Canyon right now," Barkley told reporters.

The setting for Game 3 was Chicago, and the Suns outlasted the Bulls in a triple-overtime thriller. Michael had several opportunities to ice the game for the Bulls, but he missed crucial shots and the Suns pulled it out, 129–121. After the game, Michael admitted he was tired, especially his legs. "Winning this championship is harder than anything I've done before in basketball," Michael said.

Michael's fatigue didn't show at all in Game 4 as he ripped the Suns for 55 points in an 111–105 victory. The Suns bounced back to win Game 5 and the series stood at three games to two in Chicago's favor. One more win would bring Chicago their third title.

Game 6 was scheduled to be played in Phoenix, and the match turned into a seesaw battle. With four seconds left, the Suns led 98–96. It was the Bulls' ball. Scottie Pippen spotted Horace Grant open near the basket and he fired the ball to his teammate. A two-point shot by Grant could tie it, but as the Suns' defense sagged in on Grant, the Bulls' forward noticed John Paxson alone and unguarded back behind the three-point line. He whipped the ball to Paxson who tossed up a picture-perfect, 25-foot jump shot that creased the cords. The shot gave the Bulls the victory and their third straight NBA championship.

Michael averaged 41 points in the 1993 Finals, setting a new record. He was named the MVP for the Finals a third time, too. But his team's achievement meant more than any individual record. "This means a lot to us because we made history," Michael said proudly. "We stuck together and never quit. I did my part and so did everyone."

Michael's triumph was tempered by tragedy in July 1993 when his father was murdered in a robbery in North Carolina. James Jordan was not only Michael's father, he was his best friend, and Michael was devastated. As usual, Michael turned to the strength and support of his family.

James Jordan was buried in North Carolina on a hot August day, and an audience of 200 friends and family members wept as Michael delivered a touching eulogy for his father.

Despite his sorrow, Michael tried to find something positive in the loss and he held out hope for the future. "Dad is no longer with us," Michael and his family said in a statement to the press. "The lessons he taught us will remain with us forever and they will give us the strength to move forward with a renewed sense of purpose in our lives."

Once again, Michael talked about what his father had given him. "My dad taught me to carry myself with love and respect for all."

Michael spent the next few weeks with his family, who he said gave him the strength he needed to carry on. In his first public appearance after the funeral, he told reporters, "When you have problems in your life you need to be around a good support system and these people have done a good job of supporting me. I'm doing really good, strong mentally and physically."

However, for Michael, something had been lost. The joy of playing basketball wasn't there anymore. Whatever challenges Michael had taken on had been met, and Michael now felt there was little left to achieve. And so, on October 6, 1993, just one month before the 1993–94 season was to begin, Michael shocked the sports world by announcing his retirement from the game.

"I've always stressed that when I lose the motivation and the sense to prove something as a basketball player, it's time to leave the game. I love the game and I always will. I just feel I've reached the pinnacle of my career," he told a packed news conference at Berto Center, the Bulls' training facility in Deerfield.

At the time, Michael was the NBA's fifteenth-leading all-time scorer, with 21,154 points. His 32.3-point career scoring average stood as the NBA's all-time best.

As his teammates stood behind him, some looking shocked, others looking grim, Michael explained his decision. "I've accomplished everything I set out to do. I have nothing left to prove in basketball. There are no more challenges I can get motivated for," he concluded.

Michael said his father's death had little to do

with his retiring, but James Jordan was never far from Michael's mind as he spoke. "The biggest thing I can take from my father not being here today," he said sadly, "is that he saw my last game. That means a lot."

What would he do next? reporters wanted to know. "Just relax, and watch the grass grow. Then go out to cut it," he answered.

Would he ever come back from retirement? he was asked. "The word retire," he replied, "means you can do whatever you want from this day on. So if I desire to come back and play again, maybe that's what I'll want to do. I'm not going to close that door."

Michael's fans were surprised and saddened. The *Chicago Sun-Times* ran a headline that spoke for millions: "Say It Ain't So, Michael!" But when the Bulls began their 1993–94 preseason practices, number 23 was nowhere to be seen.

17
I'm Back

Michael went to the opening game of the Chicago Bulls' 1993–94 season — as a spectator. In an emotional ceremony, the Bulls' third championship banner was hoisted up to the ceiling of the Bulls' spanking-new arena, the United Center, and NBA commissioner David Stern presented Michael with his third NBA championship ring. Then Michael sat down with his wife Juanita and his daughter, Jasmine, to watch the Bulls edge out the Charlotte Hornets 124–123.

Michael had often talked about joining the Professional Golfers Association Tour after he left basketball. But Michael surprised everyone by announcing that he would try to become a major league baseball player with the Chicago White Sox organization. (The owner of the Chicago Bulls, Jerry Reinsdorf, is an owner of the White Sox, too.)

Michael had been a star baseball player as a boy, and at age 12 he was even named "Mr. Baseball" by the Dixie Association in North Carolina. However, he had not played baseball since his senior year in high school and many doubted he could make the majors. It was one thing to hit a clutch three-point shot, skeptics said, and quite another to hit the 95-miles-per-hour fastballs or tricky curves served up by pro pitchers.

Michael began his baseball training in the winter of 1994, taking batting practice against a pitching machine under the stands at Comiskey Park. Later he took pitches from Ron Schueler, a former major league pitcher and now the Sox general manager. Michael took anywhere from 200 to 800 swings each day, five days a week.

Michael knew he had a lot of work in front of him and the odds were not in his favor. And while Michael believed in himself, he certainly lacked the confidence that came as second nature on a basketball court. "When was the last time you saw Michael Jordan nervous?" joked Schueler.

On February 15, two days before Michael's 31st birthday, he showed up in Sarasota to attend a White Sox training session at Ed Smith Stadium. So did more than 250 reporters, some from as far away as France, England, and Japan. They watched as Michael batted, fielded, and ran the bases. His time from home to first base was recorded at 3.8 seconds, faster than any other Sox player, but many observers noted that Michael's swing lacked the speed and power he would need to make it in the major leagues.

Some suggested Michael was getting an unfair break because of his fame. "Hopefully," he responded, "people judge me on my work ethic. I'm out here working hard. I'm not asking for a short-cut. I see it as a challenge."

Every move Michael made on the baseball diamond drew media attention. When he bobbled a fly ball, the TV cameras caught it. When he slipped and did a belly flop in the outfield, it ended up on the sports pages of national newspapers. Michael could also draw crowds, even to spring-training sessions. Fans flocked to catch a glimpse of Michael in a Sox uniform and he happily signed autographs for fans behind the dugout when he passed by.

On February 23, Michael went up against real pitching for the first time, not "polite batting practice pitching" as one writer put it. Facing Jose De Leon's 80-mile-an-hour fastball, Michael hit several respectable shots. He told a crowd of reporters, "It wasn't as bad as you guys thought it was going to be. I was able to make contact a little bit. I'm happy about that."

In a six-inning intra-squad game with the White Sox in March, Michael struck out twice and made a crucial error. A few reporters wisecracked that if Michael had been "His Airness" on the court, he was "His Errorness" on the diamond. Throughout spring training, Michael struggled with his hitting, despite working intensively with Sox batting instructor Walt Hriniak. In his first 15 at-bats, Michael got just one hit.

Michael was eventually assigned to a minor league team in Alabama, the Birmingham Barons. A headline in the *Birmingham News* proclaimed

"Barons Brace for Michael Mania," and more than 150 reporters showed up to watch Michael make his minor league debut. Michael quickly became the most-watched minor leaguer in baseball history.

April 8, the night of Michael's first game, was warm and breezy and more than 10,000 fans flocked to the Hoover Met, a compact concrete ballpark, to see Michael in action. He flied out and struck out twice. After the game he was asked about his hitting. "What hitting?" he responded. "I didn't hit. They told me there would be nights like this. But what I learned in basketball was that you have to have resiliency. Every great athlete has had one bad day, or two or three or more. How you bounce back determines what kind of person you are."

It would take Michael seven at-bats to get his first hit, a sharp single through the infield. The ball was taken out of play, no doubt destined to become a valuable collector's item. However, Michael went hitless in four at-bats in the next game and he continued to struggle at the plate. Later, when he made several errors in the field, a national sports magazine put Michael on the cover calling him "Err Jordan," and advising "Bag It, Michael."

Michael admitted that he was "embarrassed" and "frustrated," by his lack of progress; but when he felt that way, he said he would remember what his father would have said: "Keep doing what you're doing. Keep trying to make it happen. You can't be afraid to fail."

Still, Michael found the situation humbling. "For the last nine years," he recalled, "I had the world at my feet. Now I'm just another minor leaguer here, trying to make it to the major leagues."

Michael improved as the season went on. He put together an 11-game batting streak in late April, but by mid-season he was batting a mediocre .194.

Meanwhile on the hardwood, the Bulls had played well, if unevenly, without Michael. Thanks to Scottie Pippen's standout play, the Bulls coasted to a 55–27 record, finishing second in the Central Division. After sweeping Cleveland in three games in the playoffs, they were knocked out in seven games by the Knicks. There would be no fourth-straight NBA title for the Bulls.

Michael belted his first home run in a July game against the Carolina Mudcats. It was his 354th at-bat. "I knew the pitcher was a fastball pitcher, so I was looking for the fastball," Michael said happily after the game. "It was a great feeling."

Michael finished the season batting .202, with 114 strikeouts, 3 homers, and 51 runs-batted-in. He also had 11 errors, enough to lead the league. Later in the fall Michael would bat .252 for the Scottsdale Scorpions in the Arizona Fall League. While plenty of baseball professionals saw an improvement in Michael's skills, many more doubted he would ever have the power hitting it takes to make the majors.

A thousand fans gathered near the players' gate at the soon-to-be-demolished Chicago Stadium on September 9, a late summer day. They were hoping to catch a glimpse of Michael, who had agreed to play in a charity basketball game sponsored by Scottie Pippen. When Michael drove up in a sleek black Porsche with the AIR 1 plates, the crowd swelled and surged toward the car. Ushered into the stadium by security men, Michael suited up and stepped onto the court. He was greeted by 20,000-plus fans screaming "MICH-AEL! MICH-AEL!" and setting off enough flashbulbs to light up a small city. Michael proceeded to score 52 points in 48 minutes to beat a team led by Pippen, 187–150. Michael put on a great show, hitting long-distance shots, splitting double-team defenses to dunk on his opponents, and driving the lane as if he owned it. "He's lost nothing at all," said Scottie Pippen after the game.

Two months later, in an emotional ceremony at the new United Center, Michael's number 23 jersey was retired. With help from his children, Michael hoisted an oversized white and red banner with his name and number up near the championship banners. A larger-than-life sculpture showing Michael in flight was also unveiled in front of the United Center.

Michael, who was taking time out from his baseball training with the Scottsdale Scorpions, dismissed the idea that he would come back to basketball. "Hopefully, with that jersey up there, it will put things to rest," he said. "In basketball, I fulfilled my dream," he continued. "My dream is now to play in the major leagues."

However, that dream began to fade as the strike

by major league baseball players threatened the start of the 1995 season. As winter turned to spring, it appeared unlikely that Michael would ever make it to the majors, one reason being that there might not even be any major league baseball. On March 2, Michael left the White Sox training facility in Florida and didn't return.

Rumors began swirling that Michael, rather than become a strike-breaking replacement player in baseball, would return to the Bulls once again. After Michael worked out with the Bulls several times, the rumors grew in intensity. Just on the rumors alone, ticket sales skyrocketed in cities like Detroit and Atlanta, where the Bulls were scheduled to play later in the season. Suddenly the whole nation was watching and waiting.

Michael released a short statement on March 18. All it said was "I'm Back." It was official. Michael had rejoined the Bulls, 21 months after he left. His first game back — against the Pacers — was played in front of a national TV audience. Michael wore a new number, 45. He said his father had seen his last game in his number 23 jersey and he wanted to keep it that way. In the game, Michael looked rusty. He shot 7 for 28, and he lacked his usual speed, but he played 43 minutes and delivered 19 points as the Pacers won in overtime 103–96.

Later, Michael offered a reason for his comeback attempt. "I decided that I loved the game too much to stay away."

Michael-mania was back. A cable TV channel

ran 24 hours of Jordan highlights, a sort of MJ-TV. At the United Center, nearly 2,000 new number-45 Jordan jerseys were sold for $50 each in just four days. Nationwide, in just two weeks, souvenir jerseys with Michael's name and number outsold all the jerseys of Shaquille O'Neal, Grant Hill, and Anfernee Hardaway the previous month *combined*.

After a convincing win against the Celtics, the Bulls met Shaquille O'Neal and the Orlando Magic at the United Center for Michael's first home game. Shaq had become the NBA's top star, one whose scoring and overpowering strength and size — seven-foot-one-inch, 303 pounds — made the Magic a force to be reckoned with. Michael scored 21 on less-than-great 7-for-23 shooting, but the Magic overwhelmed the Bulls, 106–99, thanks to double-digit scoring by Shaq (24 points), Penny Hardaway (22), Nick Anderson (21), and Horace Grant (19). Grant had left the Bulls and signed with the Magic as a free agent.

If anyone thought Michael had lost his touch, they were proven wrong when the Bulls traveled to New York's Madison Square Garden to meet the Knicks. The game promised to be another exciting chapter in what had become one of basketball's biggest rivalries. Scalpers were asking $100 per ticket and up to $1,000 for courtside seats. More than 350 reporters and camera crews from a dozen countries crowded the Garden.

"The place will be rocking," promised the Knicks' Charles Oakley. "Everybody will be coming to see Michael. But everybody has played against Michael before. We know what he can do. Nothing's changed. He'll cause the same hazards on the court."

Michael wreaked havoc on the Knicks, burning them at every opportunity. He scored 35 in the first half alone, finishing with 55—one more than the Garden record he had set several years earlier. Michael was red-hot, shooting 14 of 19 from the field. He sank ten-footers in traffic, long-distance treys, fallaway jumpers, and he drove and dunked at will. In a picture-perfect play, Michael stole the ball and raced to the basket, where he dumped in a double-clutching lay-up, drawing a foul from John Starks on his way up.

With the score tied at 111–111, and just over three seconds left, Michael got the ball. He twisted and whirled into the lane and it seemed as if he would try for a game-winning jump shot. As several Knicks closed in on him, Michael fired a pass to the Bulls' seven-foot center, Bill Wennington, who was wide open. Wennington jammed it through the net for the basket and the win. The Bulls credited Michael's game-winning assist as the key to the victory.

More than 12 million viewers watched the game on TV.

Michael's presence energized the Bulls. While the Bulls and Michael took a while to get used to one another, Michael re-established the on-court chemistry he had developed with Scottie Pippen, and learned to work effectively with six-foot-ten-inch forward Toni Kukoc, who had joined the Bulls in 1993. The Bulls' record was 34–31 when

Michael returned to the roster. Of the next 17 games, the Bulls won 13.

As the Bulls prepared to meet the Charlotte Hornets in the first round of the 1995 playoffs, Michael told reporters, "Anything can happen." Michael stung the Hornets with 48 points in Game 1, a 108–100 overtime win, and the Bulls went on to eliminate the Hornets. In the next round against the Orlando Magic, Michael switched to his old 23 jersey, hoping it would bring him and the Bulls good luck. It didn't. The Bulls were overpowered by the combined Magic might of Shaquille O'Neal, Anfernee Hardaway, and ex-Bull Horace Grant. Orlando beat the Bulls four games to two. As the Magic celebrated, the Bulls sulked in their locker room. Michael sat in street clothes and talked to the press. He was disappointed, he admitted, but he added, "I'm looking forward to coming back. I still enjoy the game." As guard Steve Kerr walked by, he could see the disappointment in Michael's eyes. But he could also see something else; a look of determination that, to Kerr, said only one thing: "Wait till next year." Even though the 1995–96 season was months away, the look suddenly made Steve Kerr anxious to begin the next season.

18
A Record-Breaking Season

Michael spent much of the summer of 1995 in an intense program of weight training and conditioning exercises. He also worked on his post-up moves and his shooting, especially his fall-away jumper. When he showed up at the preseason practices, observers couldn't help but notice how much stronger and more muscular he looked.

"I heard the speculation about my age and my skills," Michael said. "All that talk got me into the gym this summer."

In October, the Bulls traded center Will Perdue to the San Antonio Spurs for Dennis Rodman. Rodman, a flamboyant and often difficult player, had been one of the "Bad Boys" on the 1989 and 1990 championship Detroit Pistons teams that had often bullied the Bulls in their meetings. But Rodman was universally acknowledged as a terror on defense and one of the best rebounders in the game. His presence would give the Bulls exactly what they would need to dominate opponents at both ends of the court.

And dominate they did from the very first game of the season. In the season opener, Michael scored 42 and Rodman grabbed 11 boards to beat the Hornets 105–91. The team won its next four games. But on November 14, the Bulls met the Magic again, hoping to avenge the previous season's playoff defeat. Instead, Penny Hardaway blasted the Bulls for 36 points, and Michael missed more than half his shots as the Bulls lost 94–88. "We'll take this one as a lesson," Michael said, "and move on."

The Bulls did so in spectacular fashion, and by the end of November, their record was 11–2. Michael scored more than 30 points in seven games, and he was as capable of his famous fourth-quarter fireworks as ever. In a November 30 match against the Grizzlies, Vancouver held a substantial lead well into the fourth quarter. But in the final six minutes, Michael scored 19 points to bring the Bulls back to win 94–88.

By Christmas, the Bulls' record stood at 23–2. There was growing speculation that the Bulls could break the 1971–72 Lakers' record for most wins (69) in a season.

Prior to a January game against the Bulls, the Philadelphia 76ers' talented rookie, Jerry Stackhouse, was reported to have said that Michael didn't seem to be playing as well as he had before his retirement. Jordan responded to Stackhouse's comments — and his defensive coverage — with a 48-point, game-winning performance that boosted the Bulls' record to 30–3. A 70-win season was looking more and more within Chicago's reach.

The Bulls had built an 18-game winning streak in early February when the Denver Nuggets handed the Bulls a 105–99 loss. Then the unthinkable happened. The Bulls lost their second in a row the next night in Phoenix. Still, by the All-Star Game break, the Bulls' record stood at 42–5. Michael, of course, was named to the All-Star team for the tenth time. He scored 20 points in 22 minutes to beat out Shaquille O'Neal for the All-Star Game MVP award.

The Bulls were firing on all cylinders and the excitement was building daily. Scottie Pippen was playing at his peak, and the Bulls were also getting strong contributions from Toni Kukoc and Rodman, who was leading the NBA in rebounding. In one game, Michael and Scottie combined for 84 points to defeat the Indiana Pacers 110–102.

By April the Bulls were 66–8, and had not lost a single game at home. No team had ever gone undefeated a whole season at home. The 1985–86 Celtics had come close with a 41–1 home record, but many Chicago fans were certain the Bulls would better that. But on April 8, the Hornets handed the Bulls their first home loss, 98–97, despite Michael's 40 points. Coach Phil Jackson rallied the team, telling the Bulls that the loss was a good reality check that would be valuable preparation for the playoffs.

Following a 98–72 drubbing of the Cleveland Cavaliers on April 14, the Bulls' record improved to 69–6. With just one more victory, they could set the new record for most games won in a season.

Was this Bulls team the best ever? Michael was asked. "We're the best this season," he responded. "That's all I care about."

On April 16, the Bulls' team bus headed north to Milwaukee for a game against the Bucks. Along the way, fans hung banners from bridge overpasses and waved as the Bulls' bus passed. A news helicopter followed above for most of its trip.

Milwaukee's Bradley Center was jammed with more than 18,600 fans waiting to see basketball history. Chicago fans who made the trip north carried signs saying 7-OH. NEED WE SAY MO'? and 70 MAKES HISTORY. The Bulls confirmed the predictions with an 88–80 win.

The Bulls finished with a 72–10 season. Michael captured his eighth scoring title with a 30.4 average and was named the regular season MVP for the fourth time. Michael's return to basketball was almost complete. Only the 1996 title was missing. "It's been a very, very long season," a weary Michael admitted after the last game, "but it can be a great season with the title." Winning the championship was both a team goal and a personal one. "I want to grab back some of the respect I lost last year," he said.

The Bulls met the Miami Heat in the first round of the playoffs. Heat coach Pat Riley urged his players to use their strength and their bodies to bully the Bulls away from the basket. Alonzo Mourning, the team's temperamental, six-foot-ten-inch center would be the key to that strategy.

Riley's tactics seemed to be effective at first, but in the second half the Bulls pulled away to win 102–85. In the next game, the Bulls blew the Heat away with a 106–75 rout. Driving to the basket, Michael strained his back in the second half, but he remained on the court for most of the rest of the game. "What we've shown," he said after the game, "is that we're smarter than they anticipated. They physically try to take us out of what we want to do. We just ignored that."

Prior to Game 3 at Miami Arena, Scottie Pippen predicted the Bulls would need just one game to end the series. "I'm only bringing one suit," he said confidently.

As the Bulls warmed up, it was obvious that Michael was hurting. He looked stiff and he winced with pain more than once. He had to lay down on the hardwood floor several times during the game to prevent his back muscles from stiffening. Still he managed to score 26 points in 33 minutes. Pippen came through with a triple-double — 22 points, 18 rebounds, and 10 assists — and the Bulls eliminated the Heat with a final 112–91 victory.

In the Eastern Conference semifinals, the Bulls faced their longtime rivals, the New York Knicks. The Knicks started strong and seemed to have the upper hand in Game 1, while all the Bulls but Michael were ice-cold, missing shot after shot, a performance that would earn them the nickname "The Invisi-Bulls" in the next day's papers. Despite painful back spasms, Michael exploded in a fourth-quarter scoring frenzy. No matter who the

Knicks put on Michael, they couldn't stop him. By game's end, he had scored 44 points to push the Bulls past the Knicks 91–84. Two days later, the Bulls' defense shut down the Knicks again, 91–80. When the series moved to New York for Game 3, Madison Square Garden was rocking. The New York fans wanted revenge and they got it. Michael tied the game at 88 with a thrilling three-point fall-away jumper at the final buzzer, but the Knicks kept the Bulls at bay in overtime and won 102–99. The series stood at 2–1.

Michael felt tired at the start of Game 4. He had played 51 minutes the night before, and his back still bothered him. He shot 7-for-23, but still scored 27. Rodman grabbed 19 rebounds and the Bulls took the game 94–91. Two nights later in Chicago, the Bulls eliminated the Knicks with a 94–81 victory.

The stage was set for the Bulls to avenge the previous year's playoff defeat as Orlando swept the Hawks and put away the Pistons, in their first two rounds of the playoffs. Magic fans were convinced that Shaquille O'Neal and Penny Hardaway would corral the Bulls once more. They got a rude shock as the Bulls routed the Magic 121–83 in Game 1. Penny and Shaq combined for 65 points, but a sustained defensive effort by the Bulls kept the rest of the Magic out of scoring range.

Plagued by injuries, Orlando still managed to take a halftime lead of 53–38 in Game 2. The Bulls' defense again turned on the heat and the Magic fell apart. The final score was 93–88, Chicago. The

Magic were losing momentum and the Bulls seized the opportunity, as they crushed Orlando in Game 3, 86–67. In Game 4, Michael dashed the Magic's hopes with a 45-point burst, ensuring a 106–101 Chicago win. The Bulls had made it to the Finals for the fourth time in six years.

The Bulls had had a nine-day layoff before facing the Seattle Sonics in the Finals, and they seemed rusty at the start of Game 1. Michael scored 18 in the first half to keep the Bulls ahead, despite scoring sprees by Sonics star Shawn Kemp. Late in the third quarter, with Michael on the bench, the Sonics tied the game and then took the lead in the fourth quarter. However, Toni Kukoc tossed in 10 straight points, and led the Bulls to a come-from-behind 107–90 win.

Michael struggled in Game 2, missing seven straight shots in the second half, but Dennis Rodman came through with a 20-rebound, 10-point performance that sealed Chicago's second win in the series, 92–88. The Sonics had double- and triple-teamed Michael throughout the game, and even though he scored 29, he felt off his usual rhythm and game. "I'll break out sooner or later," he promised.

Sonics fans came into Seattle's Key Arena loud and boisterous, but as the Bulls shut down the Sonics with a 7–0 run in the opening minutes of Game 3, they shut up the crowd. The Bulls were up by 18 at the end of the first quarter and, by the half, Michael has scored 27. In one stretch, Michael scored 15 straight Chicago points. The final score was 108–86, and since no team had ever come back from a 3–0 deficit in the Finals, it appeared certain that Chicago would take its fourth title.

But Shawn Kemp, along with the Sonics' sure-shooting guard, Gary Payton, combined for 46 points in Game 4, while the Sonics' defense forced the Bulls into turnover after turnover. Michael was held to 6-of-19 shooting, and the Sonics won 107–86. The Sonics continued to surge and won Game 5, too. The series now stood at 3–2. Suddenly the Bulls looked vulnerable.

Back on their home court for Game 6, the Bulls returned to form. Although the score remained close throughout the game, Chicago never lost control. At the final buzzer the score stood 87–75, and the Bulls had won their fourth title. As the rest of the Bulls exchanged hugs and high fives, Michael grabbed the game ball and lay facedown on the court, overcome with emotion. Later in the locker room, with tears streaming down his face, Michael was asked how he felt. "I can't even put it into words," he said emotionally. "This was for Dad. I'm very happy for him." It had been nearly three years since James Jordan had been murdered.

In a postgame ceremony, the Bulls were awarded the championship trophy. Michael, wearing a newly minted "The Greatest Team in History" T-shirt, kissed the trophy as he wiped the tears from his face. He was named Finals MVP, making him only the second player to ever win regular season MVP, All-Star Game MVP, and Finals MVP awards in a single season.

"We've got the greatest player in the world, the

greatest team in the world, and the greatest fans in the world," Phil Jackson told reporters. "We have something very special in Chicago."

Michael's comeback was complete. "I'm sorry I was out for eighteen months," he said, "but I'm happy I'm back to bring a championship to the city of Chicago." Michael was asked his thoughts about the next season. "I'd love to see this team together again to see what we could do. I don't make promises, and I'm not saying we could win eighty-seven games again, but we'd like to give it a try."

A week later *Sports Illustrated* magazine commented, "The championship trophy is the property of one man, Michael Jeffrey Jordan. He just lets the rest of the league hold it once in a while."

19
The Drive for Five

Michael faced a new challenge in the summer of 1996 — making a movie. He teamed up with Bugs Bunny, Daffy Duck, and Porky Pig to make a cartoon comedy called *Space Jam*. The movie came out in November 1996, just as the new basketball season began, and it quickly became a hit.

The Bulls got off to an explosive start, winning their first 12 games. In the fourth game Michael poured in 50 points. The Bulls' unbeaten streak came to an end in game 13 with a 105–100 loss to the Utah Jazz. Michael scored 44 in the game, then scored 40, 36, 35, and 40 in the next four games, cementing his hold on the top spot on the NBA scoring leader list.

On November 30, playing against the San Antonio Spurs, Michael scored the last of his 35 points on the final shot of the game. It was his 25,000th point. He had reached that milestone in his 782nd game. The only player to do it faster had been Wilt Chamberlain.

Chicago extended its record to 17–1, then lost two in a row against Miami and the lowly Toronto Raptors. Still the team remained the "Invinci-Bulls," racking up win after win. By year's end, Chicago's record stood at 27–4. Many fans wondered if the team would reach 70 wins for the second year in a row.

On January 8, 1997, the NBA named the top 10 teams of all time. Both the 1995–96 and the 1991–92 Bulls' squads were on the list.

Two weeks later in front of a hometown crowd, the Bulls faced their longtime nemesis, the Knicks. Pumped up by the fans, Michael was on fire. He torched the Knicks for 51 points, as the Bulls edged their rivals 88–87. The Bulls won 14 of their next 15 games to extend their record to 49–6, the same record they had on the same date in the previous record-breaking season.

Michael again was named an All-Star and his performance in the 1997 All-Star Game on February 9 was another one for the record books. His 14 points, 11 rebounds, and 11 assists marked the first time an NBA player had achieved a triple-double in the event. In a special ceremony after the game, Michael and Scottie Pippen were named two of the NBA's 50 Greatest Players.

Two days later in a 103–100 win against the Hornets, Michael passed the 26,000-point plateau. On February 16, in a game against the Magic, Michael stole the ball for the 2,113th time and moved into third place on the NBA's all-time steals leaders list. On March 3, Michael passed Dominique Wilkins, seventh on the NBA's all-time scoring leaders list, with 26,258 points. Eight days later, he passed John Havlicek to rise to sixth place. On April 6, Michael moved into the fifth spot on the list, topping the total — 26,710 — of one of his heroes, Oscar Robertson.

By the end of the first week in April, the Bulls' record stood at 66–10. They were on track for another 72-win season until the final week, when they lost three of their last four games. Still, their 69–13 record tied the 1971–72 Lakers for the second-best regular-season record in NBA history. But Michael and the Bulls knew the 1997 championship was the real goal, and the players urged each other on, saying, "It don't mean a thing, if you don't have the ring."

For the ninth time, Michael led the league in scoring, with a 29.6 average. He'd scored more than 30 points in 44 games, more than 40 in 8, and more than 50 twice. Michael had an incredible season, but in May, Karl Malone — the Utah Jazz's high-scoring forward — was named MVP. While Malone was a great player and had had a great year, many believed Michael deserved the award and that Malone was chosen to give someone other than Michael a chance to be so honored. "Michael," one Chicago writer commented, "will just have to settle for the championship trophy."

The drive for five, the quest for a fifth NBA title in seven years, began on April 25, 1997, as the Bulls prepared to defend their title against their first-round opponent, the Washington Bullets. The Bullets, a young team with talented players such as Juwan Howard and Chris Webber, thought they were ready to challenge the champs, but their hopes began to fade three quarters into the first game. The Bulls' tenacious defense left the Bullets shooting blanks, as Michael and Steve Kerr's fourth-quarter offensive attack produced 22 points to win the game 98–86.

Michael was unstoppable in Game 2, shooting down the Bullets with another high-scoring, high-energy performance. While the rest of the Bulls played listlessly in the first half, allowing the Bullets to take a 65–58 lead, Michael scored 26 points to keep his team in the game. Michael chewed out his teammates in the locker room, urging them to try harder and play their game. Michael scored 29 more points in the second half. Late in the third quarter, the Bullets' Calbert Cheaney asked Michael if he was tired. "Have we won yet?" Michael responded. "Then I ain't tired."

Michael's 55 points accounted for more than half of the Bulls' points as Chicago prevailed 109–105. "I got into that zone and I couldn't get out," Michael said after the game. "Once I got into that mode, I couldn't turn it off."

In Game 3, the Bulls found themselves down by 9 points in the last five minutes of the match. Like so many times before, Michael came to the rescue. He scored 10 of his 28 points in the final four minutes to bring the Bulls back. Then, with only seven seconds left on the game clock, Scottie Pippen clinched the 96–95 victory — and a series sweep — with a driving dunk.

In Game 1 of the second round, the Bulls overcame a 14-point deficit to ground the Atlanta

195

Hawks 100–97. Michael scored 20 of his 34 points in the third quarter to give the Bulls their margin of victory. The Hawks shocked the Bulls with a win in Game 2, as Mookie Blaylock, Steve Smith, and the Hawks' shot-blocking center Dikembe Mutombo combined for 72 points. The 103–95 loss was the Bulls' first playoff defeat at home in two years.

In Game 3, a 100–80 Chicago rout, Scottie Pippen had tried to drive to the hoop on the seven-foot-two-inch Mutombo. Mutombo rejected the shot, then waved a finger at Pippen as if to say, *No, no, no, don't try that on me.* Minutes later, Michael drove on Mutombo and slammed an amazing wraparound dunk over the center's outstretched arms. Michael grinned and waved a finger at Mutombo the same way Mutombo had at Pippen. Later Michael told reporters, "Dikembe said I never dunked on him, and I said, 'I'll eventually get you before I leave the game.' Tonight was a great time to do it."

The Hawks tried to make a comeback in Game 4, but Michael and Scottie Pippen combined for 53 points to give the Bulls an 89–80 win and a commanding 3–1 lead in the series. Two days later on May 13, the Bulls gave Dennis Rodman a birthday present by closing out the series with an easy 107–92 victory.

The Bulls looked tired in the first game of the next round versus the Miami Heat. The Heat's Alonzo Mourning pumped in 21 points, but Michael's 37 points and Scottie Pippen's 24 helped the Bulls overcome a 15-point deficit and win

84–77. The Bulls' defense held the Heat to a measly 11 points in the final quarter.

Michael played miserably in the first half of Game 2, shooting 2-for-12 for just 9 points. He wasn't any better in the third quarter, but with only six minutes left in the game, Michael found his range, pouring in 14 points to beat the Heat 75–68. The game broke the record for the lowest-scoring playoff game in NBA history. All Michael could say about his play was that it had been "an ugly performance."

Michael hit his stride in Game 3 as he racked up 34 points, but it was the Bulls' defense that made the difference as Chicago forced the Heat into a whopping 34 turnovers. The Heat were embarrassed by the 98–74 loss, but Alonzo Mourning offered no apologies. In fact, he guaranteed Miami would win the next game. He delivered, too, as Miami used its muscle and took advantage of Michael's awful 2-for-23 shooting through three quarters to win 87–80. During the game, Mourning smacked Scottie Pippen in the forehead with his elbow as Pippen rose for a layup, raising a huge bump.

As the Bulls gathered in the hallway prior to Game 5, they were ready for revenge. As they formed their usual pregame huddle, Michael told his teammates, "This one is a personal test. I want you guys to play with a lot of intensity and a lot of heart."

"What time is it?" one of the Bulls yelled.

"Game time!" the team responded. "Let's go."

Scottie Pippen injured his foot in the beginning

of the game and had to leave, but Michael made up for his absence with a 15-point first quarter and 28 points in the game. Thanks to solid efforts by center Luc Longley and guard Ron Harper, the Bulls cruised to an easy 100–87 win. The Bulls were on their way to the Finals once again. The drive for five was about to reach its climax.

The Utah Jazz had worked long and hard to make it to the NBA Finals and they were eager to face both the challenge and the Bulls. If any team had the one-two punch to match Jordan and Pippen, it was Utah. With perennial All-Stars John Stockton at guard and Karl "The Mailman" Malone at forward, the Jazz lineup had one of the NBA's most dynamic duos, plus solid sharpshooters like Jeff Hornacek.

Finals fever began to peak hours before game time in Chicago on Sunday, June 1, as the Bulls' faithful fans began arriving at the United Center. Several of them held signs urging the Bulls to STRIVE FOR FIVE.

The Bulls lacked intensity at first, but their pressure defense kept them in the game. Utah was leading 76–75 with three minutes on the clock, when Michael dodged three Jazz defenders and sank a fall-away jumper to put the Bulls ahead. A minute later, Stockton and Pippen traded three-point shots, and the score was tied at 82. Karl Malone got fouled and had the chance to put the game away with two free throws with just seconds left. Inexplicably, the sure-shooting Malone missed both shots. As the ball bounced off the rim, Michael grabbed the rebound and called time-out.

"Looks like the Mailman doesn't deliver on Sundays," Pippen cracked.

There were 7.5 seconds on the clock when Toni Kukoc caught the inbounds pass and fired the ball to Michael. Bryon Russell tried to steal the ball from Michael, but as the Jazz forward made his move, Michael saw his opportunity. He faked right, then went left with a crossover dribble. Free for a split second, Michael launched a 15-foot fall-away jump shot. Russell got a hand in Michael's face, but the shot dropped in as the final buzzer sounded. As the scoreboard flashed the 84–82 Chicago win, Jordan and Pippen hugged and exchanged high fives.

The Bulls carried the momentum into Game 2. Michael was on fire from the opening buzzer. By the second half, he had scored 20 of his 38 points, inspiring the 25,444 Chicago fans inside the United Center to chant, "MVP, MVP." Michael also grabbed 13 rebounds and made 9 assists. At the same time, the Bulls' defense stifled Stockton's playmaking ability, and forced the Jazz into 18 turnovers. Chicago won 97–85.

When the series returned to Salt Lake City's Delta Center for Game 3, Jazz fans partied in the streets, celebrating the first time the Finals had come to Utah. Inside the arena 20,000 fans raised a racket, hoping to pump up their hometown heroes. It worked. Karl Malone had an MVP-quality game with 37 points as he and John Stockton led Utah to a 104–93 victory. Two days later, the Jazz did it again, edging the Bulls 78–73 to even the series 2–2.

On the morning of June 11, Michael awoke in his hotel room at 3:30 A.M. with a headache and a queasy stomach. The feeling grew worse, and Michael's flu-like symptoms kept him in bed most of the day. A viral infection had him in its grip, leaving him feeling feverish and weak. His playing status was listed as "uncertain."

When Michael arrived at the Delta Center, Scottie Pippen wondered if Michael would make it onto the court. "I've played many seasons with Michael," Pippen said later, "and I had never seen him as sick. I didn't even think he could get his uniform on."

The playoffs had always been the one constant challenge of Michael's career, but this game appeared to be one time when he would not be able to rise to the occasion. During the pregame shoot-around, Michael sat on the bench, eyes downcast, a towel draped over his head as he tried to focus on the game.

The Jazz jumped to a 16-point lead in the second quarter of Game 5. As he played, Michael felt like passing out more than once. Sweat poured down his face and occasionally he stood completely motionless on the court.

"This is gonna be a blowout," the TV announcer told the national audience.

Michael began to gain strength midway through the second quarter, scoring 17 points in a 33-point Bull run. Despite his exhaustion, Michael rallied the Bulls, and by halftime, the Jazz's lead had narrowed to 53–49.

Michael gulped fruit juices in the locker room

and ate a few spoonfuls of applesauce, but he still felt drained and dizzy as the second half began. But Michael was not prepared to give up and he would not let his teammates give up either. He sank nearly half his shots and hit a foul shot to tie the game at 83. Then he nailed a late-game three-pointer to put the Bulls ahead 88–85. When the final buzzer sounded, the Bulls were on top 90–88. Michael had played 44 minutes and had scored 38 points. He had to be helped off the court, his arm draped over a teammate's shoulder as they headed to the locker room.

It was the kind of amazing and heroic performance that couldn't help but inspire awe in the eyes of many of his fellow players.

"The effort he came out and gave us was incredible," said an amazed Scottie Pippen. "He showed how much of a professional he is by gutting this game and staying in there. He really gave us the performance we needed and there's nothing else to say except 'He's the greatest.' He's the MVP in my eyes."

"I didn't want to give up, no matter how sick or how low on energy I was," Michael said a couple of days later. "If you give up, they give up. I thought positive and did whatever I could do. I felt the obligation to give that extra effort, so we could be here for the fifth championship."

Only two franchises — the Lakers and the Celtics — had won five titles, and now the Bulls were on the verge of becoming the third. The Chicago press was hailing Michael as "the greatest athlete of all time," and reporters were treating

Game 6 more as a coronation than as a sporting event.

Michael walked down the hallway toward the court as Game 6 was about to begin at the United Center. A reporter asked him, "Got enough to end it tonight?"

"I do," Michael replied. "I hope everybody else does, too."

The game got off to a slow start. It was 2–2 after nearly five minutes of play. The Jazz surged ahead by 10 by the second quarter and held the lead for most of the game. In the fourth quarter, the Bulls' Jud Buechler and Steve Kerr hit big three-point shots to put Chicago ahead, but the Jazz fought back and tied the game. With just 28 seconds left, the game stood 86 all. The Bulls called a time-out to discuss a play, but everyone in the United Center knew the Bulls would, as always, count on Michael. And there would be time for only one play.

Sitting on the bench, Michael leaned over toward Steve Kerr and said quietly, "This is your chance. I know Stockton is going to come over and help on defense, and I'm going to come to you."

"I'll be ready. I'll knock it down," Kerr replied.

Jordan, as expected, got the inbounds pass. Stockton, as Michael predicted, left Kerr open as he rushed over to help Bryon Russell on the double-team. Jordan rifled the ball to Kerr, who stood unguarded a foot behind the foul line. Kerr nailed the two-pointer to put the Bulls ahead for good. Moments later, Scottie Pippen stole the ball and tossed it to Toni Kukoc for a game-ending dunk.

The Bulls had won the game, 90–86, and a fifth championship.

Once again Jordan had elevated the play of those around him, and as usual, he was quick to give credit to his teammates. "Tonight, Steve Kerr earned his wings," Michael said. "He believed in himself and I had faith in him. When I passed him the ball, he knocked his shot down." Then he joked, "I'm glad he made the shot, because if he'd missed, he wouldn't be able to sleep all summer."

Michael was named Finals MVP for the fifth time. As he accepted the award, he yelled over the din of the cheering crowd, "I'll have to share this award with Scottie Pippen. He deserves it as much as I do. I'll take the trophy but I'm going to give the car to Scottie."

Pippen also had lavish praise for Michael. "No matter what's out there, no matter what there is for him to overcome, he's been able to overcome it," Pippen declared. "No matter how you look at it, he's the greatest player, the greatest one to ever play this game, and he proves it night after night."

After taking a congratulatory phone call from President Clinton, Michael was asked if he could do it again next season. "This is my fifth," he answered. "I'll do it anytime — six, seven, eight, nine. I'll do it again."

A week later, a *Sports Illustrated* article asked "Is the Jordan Dynasty the NBA's Best Ever?" Millions of fans were ready to answer yes.

Prior to the 1997–98 season, Michael signed a new one-year contract with the Bulls, worth as much as $38 million. Considering Michael's achievements, the Bulls' management and the Chicago fans were in agreement that Michael was worth every penny. With his endorsement deals, some reports said Michael could earn more than $70 million. As he had in seasons past, Michael continued his financial and personal commitment to charitable causes. Two of his most important ones are The James R. Jordan Boys & Girls Club and a Michael Jordan Celebrity Golf Classic event to benefit Ronald McDonald Houses of North Carolina.

As the 1997–98 season approached, expectations were high for Michael and the Bulls. Even before the season began, several basketball magazines were predicting a sixth Chicago title. But there were also skeptical sportswriters who said that the Bull run was over.

There certainly were dark clouds on the horizon. Phil Jackson's recent contract negotiations with the Bulls' management had been difficult and frustrating, and it seemed certain that 1997–98 would be his last season with the Bulls. Michael often claimed that he would not re-sign with a Jackson-less team, so many wondered how much longer Jordan would be a Bull.

There were other uncertainties in the Bulls' surge for a sixth title. Scottie Pippen would miss several months of the season because of foot surgery. Pippen was quite unhappy for other reasons, too. Locked into a long-term contract that left him feeling undervalued and underpaid, Pippen was demanding to be traded. The flamboyant and unpredictable Dennis Rodman was, as always, a question mark.

Michael himself had suffered a wrist injury in preseason and was not quite at 100 percent. Like the rest of the Bulls, Michael was another year older. He would be 35 in February, and he was not immune to the effects of years of wear and tear on his body. The league was filled with young, talented players whose legs had a lot less mileage than his, and they'd be eager to knock Michael and the Bulls off their pedestal.

Michael dismissed questions about his age. "Everyone says thirty-four is too old. The challenge is to still do at thirty-four what the young guys are doing at twenty-five, twenty-six. I feel I'm playing my best basketball. I feel that mentally, I know that much more. Earlier I had more reckless abandon, and was more athletic. Now I think I show more savvy out there," he noted.

If Bulls fans were expecting an easy cruise to the title, they got a rude shock in the season opener. In front of a loud Boston crowd, the Celtics capitalized on their fast-break offense, pressure defense, and 31 points from Antoine Walker to hand the Bulls their first defeat against Boston since 1992. Rookie guard Ron Mercer was treated as a hero for "holding" Michael to *just* 30 points.

"How do you stop Michael Jordan?" a Boston reporter asked Mercer.

"Nobody stops Michael Jordan, but we beat him anyway," the rookie responded.

"How do you guard Michael Jordan?" he was asked.

"You just go out there and pray that he misses," Mercer replied respectfully.

At a 30-minute pregame ceremony at the Bulls' home opener, Michael and his teammates received their championship rings. As always, Michael drew the longest and loudest cheers. The Bulls carried that energy into the game and blew away the Sixers 94–74.

Two days later against San Antonio, Michael demonstrated again that when there are just seconds left in a game, there's no better go-to guy in basketball. Michael had tied the game with a buzzer-beating three at the end of regulation. Then with the Spurs up 79–77, with just 21 seconds left in the first overtime, Michael tied the game again with a 15-foot jumper. In the final overtime, he scored three of Chicago's final four points to give the Bulls the game, 87–83.

The Bulls lost three in a row in mid-November, including a 101–80 rout at the hands of the Cavs in which rookie Derek Anderson held Michael to 19 points. The next night, Chicago's offense stalled again as it lost 90–83 on its home court to the newly renamed Washington Wizards, the same team they'd swept in the '97 playoffs. The last time the Bulls had lost three in a row had been in 1994–95 when Michael was "retired." After a loss to the Suns, the Bulls' road record stood at 0–4. The Bulls hadn't started as badly since 1983–84, the year before Michael joined the team.

With Pippen out of the lineup, opposing defenses could now double- and triple-team Michael, something they couldn't do normally. The Bulls were also hampered by injuries, and on the court they were plagued by mistakes, turnovers, and missed opportunities. The Bulls were clearly struggling and playing nowhere near the level they had the previous year. Although the Bulls were still a formidable team, their usual enthusiasm and spark seemed to be lacking. "I ain't gonna lie to you," Dennis Rodman said with his usual candor. "There's something missing and it's not just Pippen."

Thanks to Michael, the Bulls were still the hottest ticket in town. Scalpers commanded hundreds and even thousands of dollars for Bulls tickets, home or away. And when the Michael Jordan Show was in peak form, the sellout crowds got glimpses of his greatness.

In mid-November, he scored 22 points in just the first half of a 105–92 win against the Hornets. A week later, Michael poured in 49 points in a thrilling double-overtime victory against the Clippers. In an amazing performance, Michael scored the Bulls' final 9 points in regulation, sending the game into overtime. With the Bulls down by 4 with 30 seconds left in the first overtime, Michael produced a 4-point burst that tied the game at 102. Then in the final overtime, Michael delivered a remarkable 9 points — the entire scoring total for both teams — to sink the Clippers for good, 111–102.

Despite Michael's inspired performances, the Bulls record stood at 9–7 on December 1 and they were in sixth place in the Central Division. A year earlier their record had been 16–1, and the team was on its way to averaging a league-leading 103 points per game. Now the Bulls were averaging just over 87.

Despite a dislocated finger, Michael reached yet another milestone on December 9 at the United Center as he scored 29 in a 100–82 win over New York. He finished the game with 27,432 career points, 23 more than the previously third-highest scorer in NBA history, Moses Malone. Already the highest scoring non-center in history, Michael was only surpassed as a scorer by Wilt Chamberlain (31,419) and Kareem Abdul-Jabbar (38,387).

The Bulls regained their momentum in December. They won five straight in the two weeks before Christmas, including a 104–83 win against a Shaq-less Lakers team. The game was billed as a showdown between Jordan, the superstar of the '90s, and Kobe Bryant, the superstar of the future. Bryant scored 33, but Jordan pumped in 36 and, as usual, dominated the game. Winning eight straight at home, the Bulls' record improved to 17–9 by Christmas. A week later Chicago was back in first place in the Central Division.

Michael broke another record that week. In a late-December game against the Minnesota Timberwolves, he scored 33 points, making it the 788th straight game in which he'd scored in double figures. That topped the previous mark set by Kareem Abdul-Jabbar. The last time Michael had scored under ten points had been in March 1986.

Unfortunately, however, the Bulls lost that record-setting game.

Despite the sluggish start, no one was counting the Bulls out. There was still more than half a season to go. The playoffs would decide the 1998 champs, and as everyone knew by now, the playoffs were Michael's playground. At the same time, it certainly did not appear that the Bulls had a lock on the title either. With Scottie Pippen on the sidelines, team tensions rising, and Phil Jackson's coaching tenure in question, the Bulls' dynasty was looking somewhat shaky.

"When it goes, it goes quickly," Jackson philosophized. He had played on two title-winning New York Knicks teams in the '70s. He had been there and done it—he knew the score. If the Bulls were to "three-peat," or win three straight championships, twice, they faced an uphill battle, and both Jackson and Jordan knew it.

20
Sixth Sense

In January 1998, Michael was a month away from his thirty-fifth birthday. Physically, he was in great shape. Only later would he admit that he was starting to feel tired and mentally drained. He faced constant questions from reporters about just how far he could carry the Bulls, and how much longer he would play. Whatever fatigue Michael felt, it did not show as he set the tone for the rest of the season. In January alone he had four 40-point games and five 30-point games, as the Bulls boosted their record to 33–13.

Michael was on fire, and to no one's surprise, he was once again the top choice in the fan voting for the All-Star Game. "I'm happy and fortunate the fans still have me in their thoughts," he said in a triumph of understatement. "To win the most votes is very gratifying. It's a sign of respect."

In the 1998 All-Star Game, Michael put on a show, scoring 23 points in as many minutes, setting several records in the process. In a rematch of young star versus old, Michael went head-to-head with Kobe Bryant, the West's newest All-Star. Michael dazzled the fans, and challenged Kobe with outside jumpers and drives to the hoop. Kobe gave as good as he got with several clutch three-pointers and some solid ball work. The East won 135–114, and at the end of the game, the two stars congratulated each other with a mid-court handshake and hug. For the third time, Michael was named the All Star Game MVP, "All Star of the All Stars," as NBA commissioner David Stern put it.

Michael continued to reach new milestones. On March 27, 62,046 fans showed up at the Georgia Dome in Atlanta to see him and the Bulls down the Hawks 89–74. It was, by far, the largest crowd ever to watch an NBA game. Michael scored his 29,000th point on April 3 in a 41-point performance against the Timberwolves.

In what would prove to be his final regular-season game, Michael scored 44 in a hard-fought 111–109 win over the Knicks. Chicago ended the season with a 62–20 record, once again taking first place in its division. It had been another remarkable season for Michael. He had played in all 82 games, and his 28.7 points-per-game average was—for the tenth time—good enough to lead the league. Michael's career scoring average of 31.5 points-per-game stood as the best in basketball history.

In the first round of the playoffs, the Bulls disposed of the New Jersey Nets in a three-game sweep. Michael's scoring sprees—he averaged

211

more than 36 points per game—quickly extinguished the Nets' hopes. New Jersey's All-Star center Jayson Williams noted, "Everyone says he's lost something, but he hasn't lost a thing."

From the start, the Bulls' next opponent, the Charlotte Hornets, tried to stop Michael with a constant double-team defense. Even so, Michael put in 35 points and grabbed 11 rebounds to carry the Bulls to an 83–70 win in Game 1. "It never comes easy when you have to work against double teams," Michael commented after the game. "You develop a 'warrior mentality' during the playoffs."

But the Hornets' swarming double-team defense was more effective in Game 2 as Michael went scoreless for nearly 20 minutes in the second half, and Charlotte won 78–76, tying the series. After another Bulls victory in Chicago in Game 3, the action moved back to North Carolina again, much to Michael's delight.

"It's always a treat to come back home and show what you can do," he told reporters. Michael demonstrated what he could do with a 31-point effort, and a late-game scoring spurt that put the game out of Charlotte's reach, 94–80. Game 5 was an instant replay of the fourth game, and the Bulls took the series 4–1.

The Eastern Conference finals between the Bulls and the Indiana Pacers marked a reunion of sorts. Larry Bird, Michael's friend and former rival, was now the coach of the Indiana Pacers, a team full of dangerous players like Reggie Miller and 7-foot-4-inch center Rik Smits. In Game 1, Michael appeared to lose his rhythm, scoring just six points in the first half as the Bulls fell behind. In the second half, however, Chicago's defense kicked in, and then Michael sealed an 85–79 win with 8 points in the last 8 minutes of the game.

Prior to Game 2, Michael was named the NBA's regular-season MVP. It was his fifth MVP award, topping Wilt Chamberlain's four and equaling Bill Russell's five. Only Kareem Adbul-Jabbar had received the honor six times.

Once again, the Pacers jumped to an early lead in Game 2, but Michael came out shooting and turned the tide with a 41-point effort. The Bulls' suffocating defense also forced the Pacers into a string of costly mistakes, and Chicago won again, 104–98. "We've been here before," Michael said after the game, "and mental toughness is what wins this time of year."

Indiana's sure-shooting Reggie Miller was hampered by a sprained ankle in Game 3, and he was limping in pain for much of the game. He still scored 28 points, 13 in the last 5 minutes to overcome a late-game surge by the Bulls. Despite 53 points from Jordan and Pippen, Indiana squeaked by 107–105. "Today is just a bump in the road," Michael observed. "It's not over till one team wins four."

Game 4 was a seesaw battle from start to finish. Michael gave the Bulls a slim 94–91 lead with a late-game basket, but Indiana's speedy guard Travis Best took it to the hoop to make it 94–93. With less than a second on the clock, Reggie Miller took an in-bound pass, gave Michael what appeared to be a quick shove, then broke free. No

213

foul was called and Miller let fly a long three-pointer. It sailed through the net at the buzzer, giving the Pacers a 96–94 win and tying the series at two. Michael and Phil Jackson protested the lack of a call, but the referees did not budge.

"We still have to win in Chicago," Coach Bird told the Pacers, but that proved impossible. Indiana could not withstand the twin scoring assault of Jordan and Pippen in Game 5. Their 49 combined points, and the Bulls' intense defense resulted in a 106–87 rout. The Pacers managed to stave off elimination in Game 6. They were clinging to a 2-point lead with 30 seconds left when Michael sank two free throws to tie the game. But in the final seconds, Travis Best got the ball and made a quick move to the basket, forcing Michael to foul him. Best sank both free throws and the Pacers won 92–89.

The Bulls had not had to play a seventh playoff game in six years. "It's do or die," Michael announced. "We have to go out and play hard because there is no tomorrow. We're going to win Game seven," Michael assured a crowd of reporters.

The prediction proved true. Even though the Bulls shot poorly, Michael's 28 points, Toni Kukoc's 21, Pippen's 17, and Dennis Rodman's ferocious rebounding wore down Indiana's defense. The Bulls won the game 88–83, and the series. Michael reached another milestone in the game as he topped Kareem Abdul-Jabbar's all-time career playoff scoring record of 5762 by 24 points.

The Bulls were once again headed to the Finals. They were poised to pull off a remarkable feat, a double "three-peat." As in the year before, the Bulls' opponent was the Utah Jazz, who were eager for another chance to dethrone the Bulls.

It was not Karl "The Mailman" Malone who delivered in Game 1, but rather the scrappy 6-foot-1-inch guard John Stockton. His last-second shots and clutch free throws carried the Jazz to a surprising 88–85 overtime victory. At a post-game press conference, several veteran reporters who had covered Michael over the years noticed a familiar, determined look on his face, one that plainly said a second straight loss was out of the question.

In Game 2, in front of a rambunctious crowd at Utah's Delta Center, the Bulls turned the defensive pressure up a couple of notches, forcing the Jazz into making more turnovers than a bakery. The Bulls turned many of those 20 Utah turnovers into baskets as Chicago came from behind to win 93–88, and tie the series at one. Of Michael's 37 points, 13 came in the final quarter.

Game 3 was a complete blowout, a total Utah meltdown. Even the backup players on the Bulls' bench joined the scoring attack. By the end of the third quarter, the Bulls were so far ahead that Michael and Scottie Pippen got to spend the entire fourth quarter resting on the bench, their tired knees packed in ice. When the final buzzer blared, Chicago was on top 96–54. The 42-point margin of victory was the largest the Bulls had ever racked up in their championship reign. Utah's 54-point total was the lowest total ever scored by an NBA team in the playoffs.

Michael scored 34 points in Game 4, but it was an unlikely Bull who proved to be the last-minute hero. Fresh from a World Wrestling Federation exhibition wrestling match, Dennis "Rodzilla" Rodman won the 86–82 game with his rebounding and clutch, late-game foul shots. The Bulls were one game away from their second three-peat.

As Game 5 began in front of a sellout crowd at the United Center, the entire city of Chicago was ready to celebrate the anticipated win, but Karl Malone spoiled the party. Rising to the occasion, the big Utah forward responded with an intense 39-point game that carried the Jazz to a 83–81 win. If Chicago was to win the title, they would have to do it on Utah's home turf.

It seemed as if every Jazz fan in Utah had jammed into Salt Lake City's Delta Center for Game 6. The noise grew deafening, especially when the Jazz jumped to an early lead. The Bulls stayed in the game, however, and at the half, Chicago was down 49–45.

"Keep it close," Michael told his teammates in the locker room. "I have a feeling something is going to happen."

The Bulls were still behind 86–83 when they took a time-out with just 42 seconds left. In the huddle, Chicago's Randy Brown looked over at Michael and couldn't help but notice an intense focused expression on Michael's face. Later, Brown would say, "I just saw that look in his eye and knew good things were going to happen."

Phil Jackson called for the obvious play: get the ball to Michael for an outside shot, or a drive to the basket. Michael, looking tired, already had 41 points, and everyone in the Delta Center knew the ball would go to him. With 37 seconds on the clock, Michael drove to the basket and sank a lay-up to pull within one. Utah led 86–85 and only had to run out the clock to win. The Utah crowd, sensing victory in the air, raised an ear-splitting roar.

With 19 seconds left, Karl Malone clutched the ball, searching for an open man. But before he could get a pass off, Michael slipped behind him, and stripped the ball out of his hands. Malone never saw him coming. Suddenly a hush fell on the Utah crowd. Michael kept the ball in play, letting the clock run down. It was, as Michael later said, "a do or die situation."

Michael had the Jazz exactly where he wanted them. Isolated, in a one-on-one situation with defender Bryon Russell, Michael made a move towards the basket. Suddenly he pulled up short. Russell went with the fake, and with a clear view of the basket, Michael launched a 17-foot jump shot. The shot, the latest buzzer-beating, game-winning basket for Michael, was good. It was his eighth point in two minutes and it gave the Bulls an 87–86 lead. Seconds later, John Stockton's attempted three-point shot clanked off the rim and the Bulls had won their sixth championship.

"It was a long road," Michael said after the game. "Somehow we made it," a weary Michael told reporters as the team celebrated after the game in the locker room.

Two days later, tens of thousand of Bulls fans jammed Grant Park at a rally to celebrate with the Bulls. Michael pledged allegiance to the city and fans who had supported him and the team for so long. "No matter what happens," he told the cheering crowd, "my heart, my soul, and my love will always be in the city of Chicago."

Coach Phil Jackson was more direct. He knew he would not be with the Bulls in the fall. "This was our last dance and it was a wonderful waltz," he declared.

Michael had always vowed he would retire at the top of his game, and the 1998 season certainly qualified as an incredible high point in his career. Could Michael ever top that performance? Would he now finally retire for good?

Michael's decision, however, was put on hold as the 1998–99 NBA season fell victim to a messy, major-league labor dispute. The already difficult contract negotiations between the players and team owners grew impossible, and a lockout was declared. For months it appeared there would be no basketball season at all. Michael was keenly aware of his value to basketball, from ticket sales and TV ratings to sales of team jerseys, so as far as the dispute went, Michael was content to sit on the sidelines. But by the end of 1998, an agreement was reached, and the lockout ended. A new season, an abbreviated one, would begin in the new year.

Michael now believed the time had come to announce his decision. On January 13, 1999, Michael told a jammed press conference that he was retiring from basketball. "I thought about just saying, 'I'm gone,'" he joked, "but I figured I owed the fans and the media a little bit more than that.

"I tried to enhance the game and be the best basketball player I could be," he said. "From a career standpoint, I have accomplished everything that I could as an individual. Right now I don't have the mental challenges to proceed as a basketball player that I have in the past," Michael explained. "My love for the game is very strong and it's hard to give up that love," he continued, struggling to hold back his emotions. "I started when I was twelve years old and now I'll be thirty-six next month. So for twenty-four years I have been playing the game. It's sad I'm leaving the game, but it's happy because my life is starting to go into a whole other stage. It's a different challenge now and I welcome that." Michael added, "It still is a game, and the game will continue."

Michael was eager to spend more time with his family, especially his three children, Jeffrey, Marcus, and his daughter Jasmine. He also had a variety of business interests, commercial work, and charitable causes he wanted to pursue, and it went without saying that he would be working a lot more on his golf game.

Michael's last-second, title-winning shot in the

1998 Finals sealed his reputation as basketball's best player ever. No one in the game had ever made as many big shots and clutch baskets as Michael, and it's unlikely anyone ever will. But Michael has always refused to claim the honor of the best player ever to play the game of basketball, saying there is no way to compare players of other eras. As he often explained, "My opinion about the greatest player ever is that there isn't one. There have been some great players who have played in different eras. I'd like to be called one of the greatest. I never played with Wilt Chamberlain or Oscar Robertson and I won't play in whoever's era it will be twenty years from now."

By Michael's final season, however, countless fans, writers, players, and coaches were convinced, without doubt, that Michael Jordan is the greatest basketball player ever. Veteran NBA coach and Hall of Famer Lenny Wilkins, who saw Michael play and beat his teams for more than a decade, is one of them.

"No one could match Michael's skill level," Wilkins said. "I'm not afraid to tell anyone he's the best. What makes him the best is his great athleticism, the fundamentals, the knowledge, the tough-mindedness. All great pros have had tough-mindedness but he can take his up another level and I think that's unique. I've seen a lot of them, and none of them have ever been as good as him."

Some fans even venture the opinion that Michael Jordan is not just the best basketball player ever, but perhaps the greatest athlete ever.

How does Michael see himself? Michael once appeared on *Saturday Night Live*, and while the show was a comedy special, Michael offered a heartfelt and sincere view of his life.

"Pretty much of the time I'm a very happy person. I'm a blessed person. God gave me a talent to play basketball. I've been able to spread some of that talent and good feeling toward everybody and inspire other people to achieve their dreams," he said.

Despite his incredible achievements and celebrity status, Michael has remained a modest, down-to-earth man who has never lost touch with his roots. He has touched many people's lives and is able to relate to his fans whether in person or on a TV screen. Michael is a one-of-a-kind champion, yet people young and old can identify with him and his desire to win and be the best. That's what makes him a hero to millions.

"Michael could walk with kings and still keep that common touch," says Kenneth McLaurin, Michael's former high school principal. "That's what is so special about him."

"He gave us more thrills than we could ever ask for," said his teammate Scottie Pippen.

Those moments are a part of sports history. Years from now, long after he leaves the game for good, people will watch videotaped highlights of Michael's moves and swear that the man could truly fly.

Michael's longtime friend Buzz Peterson sums things up this way: "If anyone ever came into this world and was meant to be a great basketball player, it was Michael. There won't be many people to come through this life and do what he's done. He's lived an unbelievable life. It's just been amazing."

Career Highlights

- 1980–81   Leads Laney High School to Division II championship
- 1982   Gives University of North Carolina the NCAA title with a last-second jump shot; named Atlantic Coast Conference Rookie of the Year
- 1983–84   Named College Player of the Year by *The Sporting News*
- 1984   Elected co-captain of the United States Olympic basketball team; leads team to gold medal
- 1984–85   Joins Chicago Bulls; named NBA Rookie of the Year
- 1986   Scores 63 points in overtime playoff game against the Boston Celtics (April 20)
- 1987   Sets NBA record for consecutive points (23), against the Hawks (April 16)
- 1987   Sets the single-season record for points by an NBA guard (3,041)
- 1988   Named NBA MVP and Defensive Player

of the Year; wins Slam-Dunk competition second year in a row
- 1989   Wins NBA All-Star Game MVP
- 1990   Scores career-high 69 points, against the
Cleveland Cavaliers (March 28)
- 1991   Named NBA MVP, Finals MVP; leads
Bulls to the NBA title
- 1992   Named NBA MVP and Finals MVP, leads
Bulls to second NBA title; wins second Olympic gold medal as a member of the Dream
Team
- 1993   Wins seventh straight scoring title; leads
Bulls to third consecutive NBA title; named
Finals MVP; sets NBA Finals record with most
points (241) and most points per game (41);
retires in October 1993
- 1995   Makes his NBA comeback in March;
scores 55 points against New York (March
28), his 35th game with 50 or more points
- 1996   Leads Bulls to fourth NBA title; named
NBA MVP, Finals MVP, and All-Star Game
MVP; wins eighth NBA scoring title
- 1997   Leads Bulls to fifth NBA title; named
Finals MVP; selected as one of the 50 Greatest
Players; wins ninth scoring title; becomes the
third-leading scorer in NBA history
- 1998   Leads Bulls to sixth NBA title, named
regular season, All-Star Game, and Finals
MVP. Leads NBA in scoring for the tenth
time, finishing his career as the NBA's all-time
per-game scoring leader with a 31.5 points-
per-game average.

SCHOLASTIC BIOGRAPHY

❑ MP44767-X	The First Woman Doctor	$4.50
❑ MP43628-7	Freedom Train: The Story of Harriet Tubman	$4.50
❑ MP42402-5	Harry Houdini: Master of Magic	$3.50
❑ MP42404-1	Helen Keller	$4.50
❑ MP44652-5	Helen Keller's Teacher	$4.50
❑ MP44818-8	Invincible Louisa	$4.99
❑ MP42395-9	Jesse Jackson: A Biography	$3.25
❑ MP43503-5	Jim Abbott: Against All Odds	$2.99
❑ MP41159-4	Lost Star: The Story of Amelia Earhart	$4.50
❑ MP44350-X	Louis Braille, The Boy Who Invented Books for the Blind	$3.50
❑ MP48109-6	Malcolm X: By Any Means Necessary	$4.50
❑ MP65174-9	Michael Jordan	$3.99
❑ MP44154-X	Nelson Mandela "No Easy Walk to Freedom"	$3.99
❑ MP42897-7	One More River to Cross: The Stories of Twelve Black Americans	$4.50
❑ MP43052-1	The Secret Soldier: The Story of Deborah Sampson	$3.50
❑ MP44691-6	Sojourner Truth: Ain't I a Woman?	$4.50
❑ MP42560-9	Stealing Home: A Story of Jackie Robinson	$4.50
❑ MP42403-3	The Story of Thomas Alva Edison, Inventor: The Wizard of Menlo Park	$3.50
❑ MP44212-0	Wanted Dead or Alive: The True Story of Harriet Tubman	$3.99
❑ MP42904-3	The Wright Brothers at Kitty Hawk	$4.50
❑ MP45641-5	Mark Twain: America's Humorist, Dreamer, Prophet	$4.50
❑ MP45353-X	A Place to Hide: True Stories of Holocaust Rescues	$3.99

Available wherever you buy books, or use this order form.